WELSH
GHOSTLY ENCOUNTERS

Jane Pugh

GWASG CARREG GWALCH

ISBN: 0-86381-152-3

Cover: ANNE MORRIS

*First published in 1990 by Gwasg Carreg Gwalch,
Capel Garmon, Llanrwst, Gwynedd,
Wales.
Tel: 06902 261*

To my dear husband Charles Mason,
in love and gratitude.

INTRODUCTION

INTRODUCTION

It is time that I ceased for a while, writing Welsh folklore tales and delving into my collected material of Wales' ancient stories, those with the emphasis upon the supernatural. Being a Welshwoman my bias is always towards the history and folklore of my native land, and now it is time for a change; I have plenty of material, for books of Scottish, Irish, Manx and English folk tales.

In Victorian times my grandfather was the only bookbinder and bookseller in Llanrug and Llanberis and I inherited most of the stock which had been stored in my grandmother's attic. Then, I inherited all the books and manuscripts of two uncles. There were so many I gave two collections to the North Wales Universities and a collection to Caernarfon Records Office plus Caernarfon and Mold County Libraries, and still I buy books and borrow them. My tolerant family dread my going to Antique Book Fairs.

In this latest collection of the supernatural tales of Wales, I have added more stories of recent hauntings than usual. Two of them are only a few weeks old, and are, in my opinion as a journalist of thirty five years (in and outside the U.K.), newsworthy. If the sighting of one manifestation is substantiated it will be revered.

Often people, especially radio presenters, ask me do I believe in Ghosts. What can I answer? I have seen so many things (through the long years) for which no explanation can be offered. If I say "No", they think I have a cheek to write about them, but say "Yes" and they doubt my sanity.

Have my readers ever thought of someone who has been out of their minds for years, and within minutes, hours or days, suddenly heard from them or seen them? Why?

I possess extra sensory preception, which in my case usually foretells something unpleasant; very, very, seldom happiness. It is a power I personally do not appreciate. I was pleased to learn about two years ago that a Chair had been established in the para-psychological Department of the University of Edinburgh and awarded to Professor Thomas Morris of the United States of America who is a world wide expert on research into the subject of E.S.P. There is increasing interest in it these days.

Wales although small, is one of the most prolific in its fund of supernatural tales from the beginning of time. Take an easy walking route up Snowdon, when a red Summer sun is slowly sinking into the West. Look down on the dark tarns, listen to the eerie cry of the seagulls passing above your head and the hooting of the owls. Look upwards towards the summit and see if you can make out the outline of Rhita the Giant's grave. In this age-old setting, remember one or two of the stories of the supernatural you have read in this book and then say to yourself the words of the great Bard of Avon: "There are more things in Heaven and Earth, Horatio."

Good reading; try to visit the places mentioned.

Jane Pugh

A GHOSTLY REHEARSAL

In the middle of the 19th century there was a famous exorcist called the Reverend Griffiths who lived near the Llandegla Moors, near Mold, Clwyd.

Traditional tales relating to the area in which Griffiths lived always mention his success regarding poltergeists in particular. Among the many evil spirits he despatched were the Llandegla Rectory Poltergeist, the Ty Mawr, the Bryn Eglwys and the evil spirits of Ffrith Farm, Treuddyn.

He used to conjure the evil spirits, in the form of beetles or black flies, into small bottles and boxes. He weighed the containers with lead and dropped them into various sections of the River Alun.

It seems strange that there are no records of Griffiths investigating one supernatural happening near his home at one period. This was the appearance of a phantom coach which started its journey on the main A5104 road, which runs up from the Wrexham Road into North Wales. This coach would drive past the gate of Ffrith Farm, then over the Llandegla crossroads. Through the years there have been many reports of it having been seen, right up to modern times.

About the time of the start of the Second World War, a Treuddyn man claimed he had seen the coach going ahead of him. It was full of a strange light, and the coachman and an outrider appeared to be headless; it was drawn by four coal-black horses. Gliding noiselessly along, the coach would make as if to turn right for Llanarmon, then vanish.

There is another tale, many years earlier, concerning a coach at Llanarmon, but this is an account of a man's extra-sensory perception. He was totally anaware that he possessed this power.

The man, Robat ab Ifan, was riding along late at night towards his home near Llanarmon when he saw a coach travelling slowly in front of him. By the light of the moon he saw inside the coach the outline of a man who was half-lying on the seat furthest away from the driver. He did not think this unusual, but what he saw next made him begin to wonder. The coach had neared an inn where Robat used to spend quite a lot of time drinking with his friends as it was so near to his home. The coach was still moving fairly slowly and he was almost 50 years behind the vehicle when it turned as if it was about to drive into the yard of the inn.

The man speeded up his horse a little to catch a better glimpse of the vehicle but, as he passed the inn, he saw no sign of the coach. His reaction was that it was the quickest stabling of a coach and horses he had ever seen. He thought, perhaps, as he had been drinking all night, he had been imagining that he had seen a coach and rode on home as it was getting very late.

The next day he called at the inn and asked the landlord whether a coach had called there the previous night, adding: "You had that coach and horses stabled quickly, landlord." The owner of the inn assured him that no coach had called there, so Robat decided to forget about the whole thing.

Exactly one week later, to the very night when he thought he had seen the coach, he was drinking his ale at the inn when there was the sound of a coach pulling up hastily. The coachman rushed into the room saying: "Please help me, my master has suddenly been taken ill." The landlord and a few of his customers went out to carry the sick man in.

He looked pale and ill and seemed to be hardly breathing. The landlord's wife placed a blanket on an old Welsh oak settle (a long wooden seat with a high back) and the sick man was gently lifted on to it. The coachman, who was greatly distressed, was given a strong drink, and Robat ran off to fetch a doctor.

When he came back with the village doctor, the traveller was dead.

Right up to the present time there have been reports of a phantom coach having been seen tearing along the A5104. Its appearance usually takes place in the early mornings or around mid-night.

About three years ago a young woman from Treuddyn was returning home at dusk one summer evening on her motor scooter. She turned left off the A5104 up Ffordd y Blaenau. This is a long straight, but not very steep, hill up for about three-quarters of a mile and eventually leads back to the A5104 at the so-called haunted crossroads. It is possibly part of an old Roman route which goes on over the moors. Just after she turned off the main road she could see standing on the side of the road further up the hill a tall woman dressed in a long brown dress with a white or cream ruffled collar and cuffs. She seemed to be looking down the hill as if waiting for someone or something. The young woman wondered who it could be, dressed in such a strange way. As she came nearer, the air seemed icy. She rode quickly past, not being able to bring herself to look at the figure again.

Another Treuddyn lady saw a similar figure but wearing a Welsh hat standing on the same route. Again she described the air as becoming icy, although it was summer, and as she watched it, this figure seemed to vanish into the air.

Perhaps these phantom figures were watching for a ghostly coach.

A TRAGIC PROPHESY

There was a witch, or so she was called, living near Witches' Point by Dunraven Castle in Glamorganshire, during the early 19th century.

Two young men decided for a lark to visit her to have their fortunes told. One young man, Ifor, laughed at witchcraft but he persuaded his friend Dafydd to come with him. "For fun," he said.

They reached the old woman's cottage and knocked on the door. A voice called out and they knew it was the witch.

"Come in. I know you deny my powers but I will show you how great they are." They entered and were amazed.

Her furniture consisted of three three-legged stools, one table, a cauldron and a sack. Three cats sat next to three ravens on a window sill.

She told the two men to sit on the stools, then she drew a circle with a stick on the earthern floor.

"Keep listening to my voice but you must not talk."

She placed the cauldron half full of water on the fire, then dragged a sack into the middle of the room and drew out of it the carcasses of a rat, hedgehog, mole, and a skull. She threw all of them into the cauldron, and stirred the mixture while it boiled.

She chanted a Black Magic verse and gave Ifor a glass filled with water from the cauldron.

"Look through this glass at the cauldron," she ordered him. "What do you see?"

In wonder he said, "My brother in his Mate's uniform, on the deck of his ship."

"What does he look like?"

"Very ill."

"What is he doing?"

"Clinging to the mast," said Ifor, by now a bit scared.

"At midnight tomorrow at low tide go to the Witches' Point and stand alone for a quarter of an hour. Do not be afraid but take no-one with you. Come and see me the next day."

The two friends left, both very quiet, which for them was unusual.

Ifor, who was still defiant in his disbelief in witches' power, went to the Point as instructed. He had been there almost fifteen minutes when he heard a low moaning.

"Oh God, it's the *Cyhyraeth*, the death warning," he thought. Suddenly the sea began to bubble, so he left.

He saw he was being followed by a Black Newfoundland. He called the dog and when it came, patted it and tried to get it to follow him home, but it vanished. "Pity, it would make a grand pet," he thought.

He went to visit the witch next day. He said he had heard wailing and told her about the dog.

"You have seen one of the death dogs (*cŵn Annwn*). Your brother is dead."

A few days later the news came that his brother's ship had been wrecked on the Tuskan Rocks, and his brother's body was washed up close to the eastern side of the Witches' Point.

Neither Dafydd nor Ifor ever visited a clairvoyant again. Ifor lost his disbelief in the powers of witchcraft.

THE SOUL LEAVING A BODY AND RETURNING

The old Welsh folk, even up to the last quarter of the nineteenth century, believed that the soul could leave the body and return to it. The Germans believed on a parallel with the Welsh in this phenomenon, except the soul took on the form of a mouse which came out of the mouth. In Wales, during sleep, the soul was said to leave a person's body in the form of a blue light issuing from the mouth and returning through it after concluding its mission.

There were a few instances recorded of this happening in the county of Clwyd around the period of 1880 to 1893.

In Clocaenog, near the town of Ruthin, a young man courted two girls. They naturally hated each other.

One night he was spending the night with one. He looked at her lying asleep by his side. Suddenly her peaceful sleeping changed to moaning. A blue light came from her mouth. It bobbed across the room and passed through the closed wooden bedroom door.

The man threw on his clothes and followed the light. He saw it going down the garden path and making for the forest, and he walked behind it. The light bobbed and drifted at intervals through the forest. It turned to a path which led through the trees towards the home of the second girl.

To his horror he saw another light coming from the opposite direction. The two lights met and began to circle around each other like two sparring boxers. Occasionally the lights fused together. Finally, after minutes, the blue lights made off in the direction they had come from.

The young man recalled what he had heard about souls being able to leave bodies. He assumed he had seen the souls of his two lovers meet to fight for the possession of him.

When he got home the girl he had followed appeared to be in a deep sleep. He was just in time to see the blue light (which had taken a short cut to precede him) enter the girl's mouth. She woke up almost immediately, but did not remember anything about the incident.

Both girls lived for years but the young man refused to have anything to do with either ever afterwards. A few historians have written this tale in different versions. The Rev. Elias Owen was the first to relate it in 1887.

In Beaumaris, Anglesey, during 1840 a young apprentice worked for a draper who was a hard taskmaster. He was adamant the apprentices only had half an hour for lunch.

The apprentice who was the subject of this tale lodged some distance from the shop at his aunt's home.

One day he saw he was going to be late, as half past twelve was the time he was due back at work. The boy was terrified. He had looked at the clock in his aunt's kitchen and it said half past twelve, and in a few minutes looked again at the clock which said fifteen minutes past mid-day.

He raced off and was in the shop dead on time.

His co-workers said, "What have you been up to? You were here at a quarter past twelve." He put his hat on a hook and his master came in. He shouted at the boy for idling.

That night he told his old aunt about what had happened.

She said his astral body had moved out of his earthly body and gone to the shop. What the other apprentices had seen was that. It had left the shop and entered his body again to bring the earthly body back on time.

She could not explain, except that fear of his master had caused the supernatural to take over.

A woman from Oswestry was dozing in her armchair one night when she thought someone had entered the kitchen. She looked up and saw a strange blue light. She knew all about the omen of death, the corpse candle, and was terrified. Following the light was the tall figure of a well-dressed man wearing a tall silk hat. The light had by then entered a bedroom and the man went in after it. With great courage she followed. In the room was a table on which the stranger had placed his hat and gloves.

She crept downstairs and shortly afterwards the man left. The light had gone out.

Not long afterwards the woman became ill. Someone was sent to fetch a doctor, but neither of the two local doctors were home. There was a London doctor on holiday in the area, and the neighbour who had ridden to find a doctor asked him to call.

This neighbour had been told by the woman of her recent experience.

14

The doctor looked like the man the woman had seen. His actions were the same regarding the hat and gloves. There was a lighted candle on the table and in its glow the neighbour saw the body of a dead newly born baby. That, everyone said, accounted for the light the woman had seen; it was a soul light.

The woman recovered, but the tale never told whether it had been her baby.

In the early 1800s a Dr Davies of Cerrigydrudion, not far from Betws-y-coed, North Wales, was fast asleep. In his sleep he heard his name called and someone below his window say he was wanted as a woman was dying. The doctor did not get up immediately but lay listening, half awake. Again he heard the same message. He got up and went to the window, but saw no-one. The third time the message was called out loudly.

Still, the doctor did not see anyone around, but the voice said, "Come urgently to Craigeirchan Farm." The doctor knew this farm was miles away, but he saddled his horse and started on the weary journey. Not at any stage of the journey did he see anyone. It was after 2 o'clock in the morning when he arrived but he saw a light in the farmhouse window and knew someone inside was sick.

Everyone present was glad to see him, but all denied they had sent for him. No-one had left the house.

The doctor found the farmer's wife was having a difficult birth. He was able to save mother and child.

It was thought the farmer's soul had left his body and gone to seek the doctor. On foot the journey would have been too late and no-one had saddled a horse. The doctor did not believe in supernatural tales. He could not explain the voice and had never met any of the people who lived in the farm. He was certain he had not seen anyone while he was on his way.

He was left wondering, but never again was he as sceptical as formerly.

THE SECRET OF THE RIVER ALUN

About a hundred odd years ago in the small village of Treuddyn near Mold on the Wrexham side, a strange scene took place inside the old village church, according to what an old woman of ninety told me in 1978.

The Rector stood near the altar holding a tiny lead box. Near him stood a very well known exorcist and lay preacher called Griffiths of Llandegla, whose prowess at successful exorcism was known through the whole of North and Mid-Wales.

Inside the box had been imprisoned by Griffiths a small beetle, which was in a state of suspended animation.

The little church was packed and there were several people standing outside. They had come from all the surrounding parishes to see the end of an Evil Spirit. This demon had for some months been troubling the inhabitants of Llandegla and Treuddyn. It was a noisy and at times dangerous manifestation. Since it had arrived in the area, no-one was prepared to walk or ride between Treuddyn and Llandegla alone. There were numerous tales of how at night-time a massive black bull with little red eyes appeared glaring. It seemed to be getting ready to charge at the rider or foot traveller.

The demon would cause disturbances at farmhouses, hurtling things around the rooms in the dead of night, and overturning churns in the dairies. Unearthly howling could be heard in the outhouses. Stones would come hurtling out of the air as people passed the Churchyard at Treuddyn. These stones usually landed at the person's feet, but some were injured by them sometimes.

On one occasion a stone wall appeared right across a path during the night.

The Rector of Treuddyn was pressed by his parishioners to seek the help of Griffiths in getting rid of the evil spirit, and he agreed to ask him. The Rectory had been visited twice by the Evil Spirit, but the Rector had failed to drive it away from his Parish. The exorcist readily agreed, but the difficulty was in getting the Spirit into an enclosed place to prevent it escaping.

About a month after the Rector had seen Griffiths, news was brought to the Rector that the Evil Spirit was believed to be in a barn at Treuddyn on the Terrig Hill, as sounds like someone throwing jars and sacks of grain around could be heard, also a queer wailing noise.

Griffiths and the Rector quickly made their way to the spot.

They heard the howling noise inside the building, and knew the Demon was there.

Griffiths, telling the Rector to stay outside and pray, went in and immediately began reading the service of exorcism.

Meanwhile the Rector had been joined outside by a crowd of people. Inside, Griffiths continued with the exorcism which was one of the most dangerous he had ever undertaken.

Sacks of grain lifted themselves into the air and flew above his head, narrowly missing him and the snorting of a gigantic bull could be heard from outside. Afterwards, Griffiths told how the Evil Spirit had taken on several animal shapes, but he had stood firm and was unhurt. He said that he had felt himself losing consciousness during the battle with evil, but the spirit of God had prevailed against the devil, and he had revived to continue the exorcism. About half an hour after he had entered the barn Griffiths came out looking tired and shaken, holding in his hand a little leaden box. He held it up and said, "It is in this box, praise God."

After the service in church, the Rector handed Griffiths the box and together they headed a procession down to the River Alun to a section near Pontblyddyn on the main Mold to Wrexham Road. Another service was held on the river bank, and Griffiths dropped the box into the water, commanding the Evil Spirit to lie in its box on the river bed until the river ran dry.

In many ghost stories of North Wales you will read how Treuddyn exorcists in particular conjured poltergeists and demons gradually from large animals down to very small creatures such as beetles and flies, then imprisoned them into small bottles and boxes and threw them into the river.

A close friend who lives in a former farmhouse on the Llandegla side of Treuddyn tells me she can quite believe it. The River Cegidog, which is the tributary which rises on the moors and passes near Treuddyn to reach the River Alun at Pontblyddyn, flows in a loop through her garden. Through the years she has lived there, in the course of tidying up the deep river banks, and especially after flooding of the river, she has found an amazing number of small glass bottles, often embedded in the banks. Most of them are no doubt the mundane household refuse of times gone by, but some of them appear to be Georgian or early Victorian.

An interesting features is the fact that many of the bottles are found underneath the roots of a magnificent yew tree which stands above the river. (Yew trees featured in the warding off of evil.)

The ones with stoppers in place she carefully puts back where she found them, just in case!

THE BARKING DOGS

This is not a ghost story but certainly a supernatural one — an ancient tale to be found in old Welsh chronicles.

Fording the River Alun near Llanferres, about half way between the towns of Mold and Ruthin, are huge stones. The location is always known as "Rhyd y gyfarthfa".

In Welsh the bark of a dog is *cyfarth*, and the place name signifies in English more than one dog gathered together to bark.

Early in the sixth century Urien Rheged, the son of a Welsh chieftain, was walking near to the ford when he heard what sounded like the barking of many dogs, and assumed the hunt was in progress.

As he got nearer to the sound of the barking he found there was no human being in sight, only about a dozen dogs, all barking.

He had heard of the *cŵn Annwn* (the dogs of Hell) who were the hunting pack of the Underworld (*Annwn*).

Urien was somewhat apprehensive, but they seemed on his second glance to be just ordinary dogs and he made to chase them away. He waved his sword threatingly at them and this, more than scaring them, seemed to make them angry; they drew back their lips and snarled but did not move forward to resume their barking.

Glancing at the ford, which he had not intended to cross, he saw a woman kneeling down washing clothes in the river, beating them against the stones.

Suddenly she lifted up her head and he saw she was very beautiful.

He spoke to her, asking how often she came down to the ford to wash the clothes. It surprised him to see such a well-dressed woman, wearing fine jewellery, carrying out such a humble task.

When he asked her why she herself was washing clothing instead of her servants, her answer amazed him and he nearly made off quickly, but her beauty seemed to hold him spellbound.

"I am the daughter of the King of the Underworld and I am doomed to come to this ford and wash clothing until a Christian man asks me to marry him," she told Urien. "From the union a child must be produced."

19

"Perhaps this task of finding a husband may take me for ever."

Urien wondered how any man could resist such a beautiful woman, but realised she had to tell any would-be suitor who she was.

"I cannot marry you at the present time, fair one, but I will give you a child," he said. "I swear to return and marry you as soon as I am able. At present I am off to fight the English."

They made love lying at the side of the ford, and she knew that such a virile man would give her a son. Not for one moment did she think it would be a daughter; she had reached this conclusion by the aid of her magical powers.

As they parted she said, "Return to the ford in a year's time and I will show you your son."

So pleased was her father that she had carried out his wishes, he consented to her pleading that she should become a mortal to marry Urien and leave the Kingdom of Darkness until she was an old woman. Should she become a Christian he had no power to compel her to return to the Kingdom of Darkness.

Urien arrived at the ford on the appointed date and saw the lovely girl holding in her arms their fine son. They called him Owain ab Urien ("ab" is son of), and later when a daughter was born to them they called her Morfudd.

It says in one record that an itinerant monk baptised Urien and his bride, so they were never compelled to enter hell when they both died.

MORFA MINE
THE OMENS OF DISASTER

The cold winds dashed the rain into the faces of the miners, making rivulets in the dust on the toilworn faces. On they trudged making their way home after the night shift at the Morfa Mine, Port Talbot, Glamorganshire. It was the month of March, 1890 and a gloomy dawn was trying to break.

Usually the groups of miners sang to make the long trek home seem shorter.

"Come on boyos, I will start Cwm Rhondda for you," said Shenkin Evans, the local choir conductor, and started to do so. Only the odd voice or two joined in and the singing died off before the second verse.

"Come on lads, let's try Sosban Fach," urged Shenkin, but this time no-one joined him, and he gave up.

Silently they walked on, each deep in his own thoughts. So far that week there had been plenty to think about, that day in particular.

As the day shift took over the night workers found very few of their mates had turned up for the day shift. The night shift was now talking together in hushed tones. One man said to his companion, "There's strange things I been hearing this week." "Me too," was the reply.

They began going over what they had heard. Some men had said they had seen the ghosts of their dead colleagues in Number One mine. Others had spoken of the spectres of pit ponies drawing empty carts. The ponies had been led by phantom miners.

As the week progressed, rumours had spread below ground of men hearing at times the Coblynau Mine Goblins knocking frantically. These Goblins, whose actual appearance has only been recorded less than half a dozen times, knocked as a warning of disaster or the location of a prosperous seam of coal. This superstition was strongly supported by German miners during Victorian times.

During the week there had been in one section of the mine a strong sickly scent of lilies.

The final incident that gave the miners a feeling of foreboding had taken place the previous night.

As the miners approached the mine to go on that night's shift, an unpleasant sight had met them, but not supernatural. Hundreds of rats had met them, pressing on fearlessly and forcing the miners to crouch against the hedges to let the rats pass. The animals were deserting the mine.

"Oh, my God," said one man. "The mine is doomed."

Just as sailors believed that rats will desert a ship doomed to sink, the miners thought the same way about a coal pit.

The men agreed not to tell their wives. In turn the wives did not mention the Red Dogs of Morfa to their men.

These dogs ran in a pack, foretelling death in the area. They were supposed to be the hunting dogs of Satan, and their Welsh name was *cŵn Annwn* (Dogs of Annwn, King of Hades).

The men continued their homeward journey in silence, and it was fully daylight when the last one entered his house.

Margaret Jones and her next door neighbour, Sharon Evans, were chatting. Sharon, a very young newly-wed, a stranger to the area, was about to set off for the local shop; Margaret, a fifty-eight year old widow had been scouring her front door step.

She said, "Did you hear them dratted dogs last night running up and down the street howling? They been doing it all week."

Sharon said she had heard them.

Margaret wiped her soapy hands on her sackcloth apron and settled down to tell the newcomer all about the Red Dogs of Morfa.

After listening as patiently as she could the girl said, "Red dogs, rubbish! I wish silly people would keep their bitches in, disgraceful it is, packs of dirty old dogs chasing them. Keeping us awake," and she gave a little giggle.

"Believe what you like, Sharon, but do not be laughing at me. I tell you, seeing and hearing them dogs means death," was Margaret's reply.

"Whose death?" was Sharon's answer.

Now Margaret was really annoyed at being laughed at and said huffily, "How should I know, you silly girl."

Just then, along came another woman of about sixty from the next street whose name was Nansi Thomas.

Margaret told her about the Red Dogs of Morfa and how

Sharon scoffed at the tale. Turning to Sharon, Nansi said, "Oh! It is true, bach. Those nasty dogs were howling their heads off last night and Mari Hughes, who was in our house visiting me, and I heard the sound of their feet. We was both afraid of peeping through the window curtains even."

At this point Margaret started on what promised to be a marathon story of what had happened on different occasions through the centuries after the dogs had been seen and heard.

The girl decided it was time to be off. "Do enjoy frightening yourselves," she said, and made off briskly towards the shop.

"Full of sauciness is that one, but she will learn," remarked Margaret, and the two women turned to watch Sharon walking away.

During that week some of the older miners swore they had seen corpse candles moving slowly along the seams, giving a blue flickering light. The Welsh tradition was and still is in some isolated country places that they were sure Omens of Death. Anyone who saw a corpse candle would die within a week. The alternative was that a relative or close friend would die.

It was the account of the departing rats that made many of the day shift leave the mine. They knew they would be sacked, and it would be almost impossible to obtain work without leaving the area, but this did not prevent them going back home. So strong was their superstition that they were quite convinced something dreadful was about to happen at the Morfa mine.

That day, the 9th March, about noon, their premonition was proved true.

With a dreadful sound of thunder part of the Morfa Mine collapsed, killing eighty-seven of the miners.

In the Morfa area there are even up to today a few old men over ninety who say that when they were very young children they can remember hearing the noise of the mine collapsing. They speak of fathers, grandfathers, uncles and big brothers who never came home again.

Nearly every family in the village lost someone during that week of omens, and the story of the Morfa Mine will live forever in the history of mine disasters in Wales.

HAG OF THE MIST

No book on the Supernatural in Wales would be complete without an account of a meeting with the fearsome phantom known as *Gwrach y Rhibyn*, Hag of the Mist.

Through the centuries no more than three accounts of the sighting of this supernatural being have been recorded in the County of Clwyd, North Wales. There are many stories of its appearance in other Welsh Counties. In all these tales the description of the evil spirit is very similar.

Skinny, with long arms, long straggling hair, hideous black fangs and leathery huge batlike wings, the Gwrach could take on male or female sex at will.

Most times it is said to manifest as a female.

It was supposed mostly to visit (unseen) a house where a person was dying. In the still of the night it was heard to beat on a window with its wings and howl the name of the person about to die. Other places it haunted were marshes, mountain sides and the edges of lakes.

One of its favourite pastimes was to frighten travellers at night or in the mist. In a seemingly terrified voice it would call out, "Oh my children!", or "Oh my husband!", or "Oh my wife".

People hearing it would run in the direction of the voice to give help. If they ran up the mountain they fell over the edge in the mist to their deaths, or else they drowned in the lake as they tried to hurry through the lowland mist.

A man living near Caergwrle, which is between Wrexham and Mold, was one evening in 1868 making his way home along a very lonely path about two miles from Wrexham. After spending a merry evening at a Wrexham Inn he was slightly unsteady and stopped for a rest.

Three times he thought he heard a large dog howling, the howl getting louder and more piteous in tone. Looking around in the semi-darkness he could not see the shape of any cottage or farmhouse, but the howls had sounded quite near. It became dark suddenly and he heard a queer heavy clapping sound coming from almost above his head. The next thing he heard was a blood chilling shriek, the flapping noise increased, and a black creature dropped down beside him. It landed on all fours.

In his terror he could not even scream, let alone pray; he just stood still, waiting for (he was certain) death.

The moon came out and he was able to see the horrific thing was female. He knew it was a Gwrach y Rhibyn.

Nearer and nearer she crawled, her great bosom protruding in front of her. Long black teeth grinned at him, and long bony fingers reached towards him.

"Come, lovely man," she crooned.

When the dawn came he was found still lying there by some farm workers. By his babbling about black wings and long black teeth, the men thought the man must have seen the dreaded Gwrach y Rhibyn. They half carried him to the Rectory. The Rector recognised him as Meurig ap Tomos, a jovial fellow, fond but not immoderately so, of his ale. After he had heard what Meurig was supposed to have seen the Rector blessed him and said prayers.

Formerly glowing with health, Meurig's condition deteriorated quickly, and within three months of the incident he was dead.

In the early part of the eighteen hundreds a Beddgelert man met a Hag of the Mist on his way home. He too died within a few months of seeing the spirit, which was also in that case female.

THE LLANIDLOES POLTERGEIST

The household at Graig Wen Farm were very popular with all the people who lived in the vicinity of the farm in Llanidloes, Mid Wales.

In the past many a *Noson Lawen* (Merry night) had been held at the farm. These had at times attracted travelling poets and clog dancers from outlying districts.

The singing at Graig Wen's Noson Lawen was in the true Welsh tradition of that part of the early nineteenth century and the beer was strong and plentiful.

Now there were no longer any festivities at the farm and there were few visits made by the neighbours. This was all on account of a very unwelcome visitor, a poltergeist, whose mischief kept them away.

In those days the Welsh believed strongly in the supernatural but not many of them believed in tales of the *Tylwyth Teg* (The Fairy Folk).

In most accounts of poltergeists, past and present, there seems to be a young person living in the house, who is in his or her early teens.

In the case of the Graig Wen haunting, the poltergeist first turned its attentions to a fourteen year old girl servant named Olwen.

One day the girl swore she saw a mouse sitting in the corner staring at her and then grinning horribly. The idea of a mouse sitting grinning at anyone set the whole household laughing and teasing the girl unmercifully. As if angry Olwen had told about the mouse, the poltergeist started slapping her in the face and pinching her. Alarmed by these attacks, which became frequent, she left her employment at the farm. On the day she left there was a disturbing scene and the farmer's wife went in to see what was wrong.

"It is just your imagination *Cariad Bach* (little dear)," the farmer's wife told the frightened girl, but felt rather uneasy herself, and she did not persuade the girl to stay.

Now that Olwen had left the farm the poltergeist turned its attention mostly to another fifteen year old girl servant, Menna. It was quite gentle with her and according to her, used to touch her face lightly and it hit her once or twice with something like a soft feather pillow.

Sometimes, heavy pieces of oak furniture moved a foot or os by themselves.

The Evil Spirit was not quite so violent for a time and pots and pans floated in the air at mealtimes just above the heads of the eaters at the big farmhouse table in the kitchen. Soon its mood changed suddenly and at night it could be heard screaming with laughter around the house. By now all the girl servants were all sleeping in the same room.

Out in the stackyard the men servants and male members of the farmer's family were kicked on the shins hard and milk churns were overturned.

This was getting all too terrifying for the servants, male and female, and they asked for their release from their annual contracts. For protection they had made small wooden crosses which they always carried about with them.

After persuasion from the farmer and his wife, they agreed to stay a little longer on condition that the farmer obtained the services of an exorcist.

He said he would and arranged for the Vicar of a nearby Parish, who was famous for his exorcism, to conduct a service at the farmhouse.

It was as if the Evil Spirit knew what was to happen and while everyone waited for the exorcist the poltergeist turned its attention to the Bibles in the house. Any Bible it found in a room was hurled around so hard it damaged dishes and knocked ornaments off tables and shelves. The largest and heaviest Bible in the house was kept in the kitchen where short prayer services were held each night by the farmer. The services called *Dyletswydd* (Duties) took place all over Wales in every home.

It was during the next nightly service after the farmer's visit to the exorcist that this Bible was tossed around the room. It travelled past the faces of the terrified people in the kitchen.

One night no one could sleep, doors were slammed; chests were banged open and clothes were flung about. Screaming and hooting echoed all around the house, and continued at intervals until cock crow.

It was to their credit the servants did not leave the next morning, but they knew the terror could not last much longer and they liked their employer, a God-fearing and kind man, so they stayed.

That evening, the Vicar arrived carrying a big handbell, a candle and a Bible. He had begun the service of exorcism whilst still outside the farmhouse kitchen door, ringing the bell and reading from the Bible. This was the signal for all the household to go outside, only the very brave peeping through the window.

Once inside the Vicar put down the bell and lit the rush candle, placing it on the floor near him. He read aloud passages from the Bible used for exorcism. He rang the bell with its left hand while holding the Good Book in his right.

Suddenly, came a rush of wind extinguising the candle. With the wind came a howling noise like that made by a huge hound. Calmly, the Vicar relit the candle and continued with a passage. He stopped reading and called loudly, "By the most Holy name of Jesus, I command you foul fiend to return to Satan and leave this household in peace."

In answer came a Satanic peal of laughter and the farmer's Bible left the table it was on and came straight for the Vicar's face. He did not flinch; again and again this manoeuvre was repeated, but the Vicar went on reading.

Now he commanded the Evil Spirit to manifest itself in its true form.

There appeared in the centre of the kitchen, the figure of a young man, his face twisted with evil. He wore very fashionable Georgian attire and in his hand was a sword stained in blood to the hilt.

The spectre ran at the Vicar, the sword pointing at him. The Vicar did not move.

"Return to Hell by the Power of the Holy Trinity," he said sternly, pointing at the spectre. The Spirit dashed out of the room howling pitifully as it went.

Its reign of terror was at an end and the family and servants of Graig Wen Farm came back into the kitchen, and with the Vicar they all knelt and thanked God for their deliverance from the Evil Spirit.

"WAS IT AN EVIL GIFT?"

Geraint ap Gwilym (*ap* — son of), an eighteen year old youth, lived alone in a small farm near Betws-y-coed, North Wales, during the latter part of the eighteenth century.

He was fond of visiting relatives and friends as often as possible. The farm he lived at was isolated and dreary.

Most of these visits were to the Denbigh area of Clwyd. Summer or winter he used to start off on his journey before dawn. This was because he wanted to visit as many houses as possible for a chat and a sup of ale.

To reach his destinations it was necessary for him to cross the Denbigh Moors which for centuries was supposed to be peopled by ghosts, goblins and hags of the mist, all waiting to scare travellers.

He was not of a nervous disposition and had laughed many supernatural tales to scorn. There was only one thing he was scared of, and that was being set on by robbers. It was thought the Red Banditti from Merioneth had at times been near his home, but they lived over forty miles away.

As a measure of protection Geraint always took with him a stout stick made of Welsh black oak. He knew several prayers for his protection and frequently repeated them as he walked.

One cold winter's morning on the edge of daybreak he set off on one of his usual visits. The moor that morning looked even more bleak and uninviting when the day fully broke, although there was a little wintery sunshine.

After walking about three miles along the moorland he felt a strange feeling of weakness coming over him; something he had never experienced before. The feeling increased and made him almost feel nervous.

Geraint stopped and it was then he felt someone near him, but on looking round there was no-one in sight. Thinking it was because there was not a soul around (he couldn't even see a sheep) that was causing the unusual feeling, he decided to sing for company. He knew not all Welshmen are singers despite the English always saying they were. He started walking a little more briskly than before.

It was then he noticed someone coming towards him and he

wondered a little where the figure had come from because when he had stopped to look around there had been no sign of any person anywhere on the horizon. This did not really bother him, as he was pleased that at last there was someone he could chat to for a short while.

As the figure came nearer he was able to see it was that of a very tall gentleman, dressed in the height of fashion, who was wearing a tricorne hat. He started to wish the stranger good-day, but stopped after the first part of the greeting.

The gentleman was really close so that Geraint was able to see the figure had a black gap where his face should have been.

At that moment, Mot, his dog who was with him, and by no means a timid dog, raised his hackles, snarled fiercely and began to howl.

The stranger took one step forward and the dog fled, howling piteously. As for Geraint, he found himself unable to move one step backwards or forward. On and on came the stranger and Geraint thought he would crash into him, but he still could not move. He had no need to, for the figure passed straight through his body.

As this happened a pain shot through Geraint's spine from top to bottom, and immediately he found he was able to move again.

Could it really have happened? It must have, as the pain had been very real, the youth thought as he turned for home, running madly. Ahead of him he could see Mott in the distance and the dog was still howling.

It took him over a month to finally convince himself he had been daydreaming and perhaps moved awkwardly to cause the pain, so he decided one morning to take the same route across the moor to visit members of his family.

Conditions on the moor were the same as they had been on his last journey across them. He did have a slightly uneasy feeling when he reached the spot where he thought he had met the faceless stranger.

He looked down and there at his feet lay three golden sovereigns. He was amazed and bent down to pick them up, but changed his mind and decided to leave the gold alone. Geraint had heard tales of Devil's Gold with which Satan paid for the souls of persons. It could be, he thought, that if he picked up the gold the Devil might appear next time in his full Satanic majesty and bargain with more gold for his soul.

In spite of the fact that he was afraid the Devil or the ghost might appear in another guise to persuade him to take the gold, he said a few prayers and went on his way.

Geraint ceased to cross that part of the moor again to reach Denbigh, and his relatives and friends were puzzled why he now took so long to reach their homes. He told one or two of them why he was using another route. Those he told had to put their hands on the Bible and swear never to repeat what Geraint had told them of his dreadful encounter on the moors.

Another old Welsh folk story tells how another man had a similar experience quite near where Geraint had met the gentleman with the tricorne hat.

In that case he collected avidly for years the very welcome gifts of gold and jewels left at the spot. He lived until he was very old and left all his wealth to the Church, so the old folk story-teller recorded.

LAND FOR THE POOR

The wife of Dr Bretton, Rector of Pembridge, near Hereford, a kind and religious woman, died in the last year of the seventeenth century. Her charitable works were known throughout the whole parish and the news of her death was received sorrowfully.

Apart from her husband (the Brettons had no family) the one who missed her most was her former maid, Alice, in whose welfare the late Mrs Bretton had taken a great interest.

With Dr Bretton and Mrs Bretton's blessing Alice had married a young groom on a nearby estate about half a mile from the rectory, where she was able to still continue helping at the Rectory. After Alice had been married about two years she had a baby girl and it was a few months after the birth of the baby that Mrs Bretton died.

One night shortly after her mistress' death Alice was sitting in the kitchen of her little cottage rocking the old wooden cradle where the baby was fast asleep. Her husband was away with his employer selecting horses.

Since her marriage she had never been alone overnight and was slightly nervous when she heard a gentle tap on the door. After hesitating for a few minutes she opened the door. There stood a lady who was a replica of her late mistress.

Alice said, "Oh, ma'am, if I did not know my own dear mistress was dead I would think that you were she. You look so alike."

The lady replied, "Alice, my dear, I was your mistress. This is my unquiet ghost you see before you."

She caught Alice's hands in her own. Her grasp felt so icy it seemed to burn the girl's hands and this frightened her. She was even more frightened when the spectre asked her to come with her on a matter of great importance.

Alice said, "I am truly sorry, dear Mistress, but I cannot possibly leave my little baby alone at night. She might wake. Perhaps it would be better if you called on the Rector and asked him to go with you."

The ghost replied that Alice was the only one she wanted to accompany her but that she would share the secret with her late husband, the Rector, afterwards. The ghost assured Alice the baby would sleep soundly until she returned to her little cottage. After a lot more pleading the ghost finally persuaded Alice. Carefully tucking the sleeping baby warmly in the cot Alice gave the child a light kiss on the forehead, then she slipped on her cloak and left the cottage with the ghost.

Together they climbed a stile which lead to a large field and the ghost, moving away from Alice, began to pace out the measurements of the field. The ghostly footsteps eventually covered over three-quarters of this field, with Alice trailing behind her late mistress.

"I know you are very weary, Alice, but have you noted the area of the land I have walked on," said the ghost.

The girl, who was almost asleep on her feet, said that she had.

"Now, Alice, all I have measured tonight of this land belongs to the poor of this parish, to whom it was willed by an uncle of mine. My brother and my late father made a false statement about this land and told the notary it was my land.

The ghost went on to say that the Rector had not been told of the deception so that after the death of their father only she and her brother knew about the wrong done to the poor of the parish. The spectre told the girl that next day she wished her to call on the Rector and explain about the wrong, and the Rector would make her brother give the land to its rightful owners.

The girl agreed to do this and then being terribly anxious about her baby asked the ghost to let her go home at once. The ghost accompanied Alice home and the girl was delighted to find her little baby did not appear to have even stirred and was sleeping peacefully.

The two talked for a while and then before disappearing Alice's late mistress said, "Goodbye, my faithful Alice, you will not see me again in this world if you carry out my instructions and I shall lie quietly in my grave."

Next morning Alice left her baby in the care of a neighbour and went to see the Rector, who was not at all surprised to learn she had been visited by the ghost of his dead wife. He asked her to accompany him to see his brother-in-law.

When they told him Alice had seen his sister's ghost who sent him a message to give land to the poor, he said the girl was talking nonsense. When Alice revealed the secret that only the ghost and he knew, he became very upset. He was afraid that if he did not carry out the ghost's wish he would be haunted by the spectre for the rest of his life, as he had heard of such things happening. He told the Rector that he would see the land was handed over to the poor of the parish immediately. The Rector made sure his brother-in-law kept this promise. The land was sold for a high price and the money used by the Rector to help the poor people of his parish.

THE HAUNTED FARM

There is a farm called Ffrith in Treuddyn, Clwyd, which stands a little way off the Corwen Road, and the old farm and the path leading to it were through the years, and still are, the subject of several haunting stories.

Round about the middle of the 19th century the first manifestation of evil was reported.

One morning two of the dairy maids were making cheese when they heard a howling noise outside the dairy door. Suddenly, it was thrown open by an unseen hand and a quantity of mud and filth was thrown amongst the curds. The girls ran out in terror to tell the farmer and his wife what had happened.

The wife asked her husband if the farm had been visited by a witch begging for vegetables or other goods and he said no, but asked her if she had refused clothing or anything to any old woman who looked like a witch. The farmer's wife and the servants said no-one had been to the farmhouse to ask for anything.

It was the time of the century in Wales when Witches were said to cast a spell on the churning.

Now the farmer after hearing no old woman had visited his farm, felt sure an Evil Spirit was in or around the place. Things became very uncomfortable in the farmhouse itself. Objects whirled around the kitchen during the night and when the household got up in the morning they found food thrown all over the kitchen floor.

Then the poltergeist became tired of causing damage and disturbance in the house. It started once again to visit the dairy. When anyone tried to churn, an unseen force seemed to prevent the churn handle from turning. While milk was being cooled in large earthenware pans on the slate shelves of the dairy, pieces of slate, twigs and lumps of moss were thrown into it. Life by then had become frightening and intolerable for both the family and the servants.

Things came to a head when a young milkmaid, braver than the rest, tried her hand at churning. She fancied the churn handle was beginning to move and turned it a few times, rather gingerly. While she was doing this, her cap was snatched off her head, the strings became wrapped around her throat and pulled tight, with the result she had to be rescued by the other servants.

Now the farmer knew something had to be done quickly as the prayers of the household had no effect upon the poltergeist. He sent servants to the village stating that he would give five golden sovereigns to anyone who could successfully exorcise the poltergeist. A Priest who lived in the locality heard of this offer and told the farmer he would exorcise for ever the Evil Spirit of Ffrith Farm. A few days after making this promise, he arrived at the farm with his Bible.

He went into the kitchen and started to read from James, Chapter Two, the Nineteenth Verse, "The Devils believe and do tremble". This was followed by an extract from John, Chapter Three, "For this was the Son of God manifested that he might destroy the works of the Devil."

This had violent results. Things began to happen in rapid succession. His own Bible was snatched out of his hands; the family Bible rose up off a table, and both Bibles hurtled round the room. One Bible struck him three or four times on the head while the other whirled back and forth in front of his nose.

He managed to make his way out of the kitchen to join the crowd waiting in the farmyard. He looked in a dreadful state with two black eyes, and when his coat was taken off it could be seen he had several bruises on his arms. His legs were also badly bruised.

The Priest told how he had been battered by the Bibles and kicked by the unseen poltergeist. He was telling the assembled people all about his experience when a shower of stones came towards him and he took to his heels. Nothing would induce him to come near the farm again to try another exorcism.

One strange aspect of the whole incident was that none of the stones struck the terrified onlookers.

Some of the servants left their employment that day and others gave in their notice.

The night following the attempted exorcism there was more banging than ever and bed-clothes were snatched off the servants' beds. Two of the men servants said they had felt something like a cobweb brushing across their faces while they lay in bed. All through that night, the house was filled with a terrible wailing. In the morning the members of the household all felt a sensation as if cobwebs were barring their way to the kitchen, but there were none in sight.

The farmer was desperate, as he was about to lose all his workers and the harvest time was approaching.

He had heard of an exorcist called Griffiths who lived nearby at the village of Llanarmon-yn-Iâl, who had succeeded in exorcising Evil where Clergymen had failed.

He rushed off to see the man, who promised to help. He arrived at the farm within a few hours, carrying branches of yew and rowan and a large box.

As before, the farmyard was crowded with spectators, but after the last unsuccessful attempt at exorcism, they all kept well away from the house.

The exorcist once inside the house formed a circle with the yew and rowan branches. Then he opened the box, took out some salt and sprinkled it in a circle inside the one he had made from the branches. He stepped into the circle, and taking a Bible out of his pocket, started to read the same passages as the Priest had done. He soon realised that the Spirit he had to exorcise was one of the most powerful of its kind. He thought it would take on large animal shapes and that the barn was the best place in which to exorcise it. Greatly daring, as the poltergeist could have manifested at any time, he carried his Bible, branches and the box of salt out of the house and went into the farmyard.

"Have you finished already, sir?" asked the farmer.

Griffiths explained that the Evil Spirit could take on very large animal shapes and he needed to go to the barn to carry out the exorcism. At the same time he warned the farmer to keep the onlookers well away from the barn while he was dealing with the poltergeist.

The crowd was more than willing to obey these instructions, as they had seen a ball of fire following Griffiths from the house, and most of them had already backed outside the gate.

The exorcist was aware he was being followed by the ball of fire, but he pretended not to notice and entered the barn.

He set up the two circles and started to read from the Bible, then he heard the sound of loud breathing which changed into a snorting, followed by a bellowing, and there outside the circle stood a huge black bull with glaring eyes. The exorcist carried on reading and the shape changed into a tiger with green eyes and a swishing tail, making a rush towards Griffiths who still carried on reading.

The horrified crowd heard banging, bellowing and howling coming from the barn, but above all the noise, Griffiths' voice could be heard commanding the Evil Spirit to change it shape to that of smaller animals.

They heard next the bleating of a goat and were afraid that the Devil himself, whose favourite shape was that of a Black Goat, had come into the barn to assist the poltergeist, and all feared for Griffiths' safety. They fell on their knees and prayed to God to save Griffiths. Before long all became quiet and then the barn door opened, which made them rush back to a further place of safety.

Out of the barn came a tired but triumphant exorcist, carrying in his hands a small bottle. Holding it up he said, "Look at this black fly in the bottle. It is the Evil Spirit which will trouble Ffrith Farm no more."

Putting the bottle into his pocket he walked off.

No-one knew what he did with the bottle and its prisoner.

Some twenty years ago one or two old people living in Treuddyn told the Author of this book how their grandparents had related the story to them, saying that Griffiths had taken the bottle, placed it in a small iron casket and buried it in a river bank somewhere in the area. He had commanded it to remain there for a thousand years.

For many years there were no more talks of haunting at Ffrith Farm, until the early part of this century when in 1928 there were reports of poltergeist activity at the farm, and rumours of a headless grey horse cantering up the path leading to the farm and disappearing into a hedge.

THE WARNING SPIRIT

For almost 200 years a spirit was supposed to frequent the church at Llangernyw in Clwyd. It was not a troublesome spirit and most of the year it kept very quiet, but occasionally it delivered a warning to individuals in a blood-chilling whisper. Only the recipient heard the warning.

The whisper was not a threat, but sometimes it told of the danger of flooding or it told the man or woman hearing it of impending disaster and of how they could avoid this.

The spirit was given the name "Angellyston".

On All Hallows Eve it became a prophet of doom in the most awesome manner. On the first stroke of midnight, should anyone be bold enough to stand outside the east window of the church, they would hear the spirit announcing the names of the parishioners, young and old, who were to die before the year was out.

There appears to be only one record of anyone having heard the dread announcement of his death.

It would appear from research that many people did find the courage to listen at the east window, but they kept extremely quiet as to whether they had heard their own or other people's names called by the spirit.

A local tailor named Sion ap Robat (John, son of Robert) was very sceptical about the existence of the spirit and he stated that, if there was one, it certainly did not possess any powers.

On All Hallows Eve in 1890 he said to his friends: "There's fools you are believing in a silly old spirit, and I am going to prove to you this night there is no spirit.

"I will go to the east window of the church at one minute to midnight; there will be no ghostly whisper, just the sound of the night breeze moving through the churchyard trees. Afterwards you can buy me some spirits out of a bottle," and he laughed loudly.

True to his word, he set off that night in the company of his friends to the church. They did not go up to the east window with Sion, but stood in the churchyard making sure they were out of hearing, just in case they heard their own names called.

It was one minute to midnight and Sion stood underneath the

window, and right on midnight he heard a terrifying whisper.

It said: "I call on Sion ap Robat to yield up his soul to God or Satan on —."

The man did not wait to hear the date of his death, but turned away shouting: "No, no spirit, I am not ready."

He ran towards the churchyard gate, pushing aside his astonished and fearful friends.

Sion was not seen again that night but, a few days later, his friends met and questioned him. He denied at first that he had heard his name called by the spirit. They reminded him that he had called out he was not ready; in view of this he had to confess how he had heard the spirit call his name.

"Pack of old rubbish," he said scornfully, making for the inn.

It seemed as if the spirit's prophecy had not been correct as, on the last day of that year, Sion ap Robat was still alive and was at a party celebrating with his friends the fact that he was still alive.

Two minutes before the New Year came in the tankard of ale fell from his fingers and Sion, a hale and hearty man of 40, collapsed to the floor dead.

THE BWCA

In the cottage nestling beneath the shadow of Snowdon, the little maid-servant, Nansi, sat knitting a stocking. She huddled closer to the peat fire burning in the huge fireplace on that very cold January night, during the fifteenth century.

Her employer, Farmer Huw Evans, his wife Margiad, his two sons and a daughter, together with some of the farm servants, were away at a *Noson Lawen* (Merry Night) held in a farm about a mile away. Evans' farm was called Trwyn.

Nansi had promised to finish the pair of stockings for her *Nain* (grandmother) and had decided not to go with the others.

"*Bobol bach* (Dear me), there's a cold night it is," she thought, and drew even closer to the fire, at the same time clutching her woollen shawl tighter around her shoulders.

Suddenly, she lifted her head from her knitting as she heard a shuffling noise in the room. Surely she was imagining things, because she felt certain the old Welsh Dresser moved slightly.

"There's silly I am, to be sure," she mused, and started to count the stitches, because she thought she had dropped one.

Before she could finish counting, the noise came again, and to her terrified eyes the dresser seemed to move again, this time a few inches to the left. With a scream the girl jumped up, knocking over the stool she had been sitting on. Instantly the stool was picked up and hurled across the room to the accompaniment of sinister laughter. Nansi just managed to save herself from fainting and staggered to the door, accompanied by the sound of the laughter.

Once through the door she fainted and was found some minutes later by the returning revellers.

"Girl, girl, what has happened?" asked the farmer's wife.

The girl was in no state to tell them anything for at least half an hour.

At last, she stumbingly told them about the dresser moving and the stool being hurled about to the sound of hellish laughter. None of her hearers laughed, because this was at the start of the fifteenth century, and no-one disputed the existence of what we now call poltergeists.

It took them a long time to persuade Nansi to stay on at the farm. She was an orphan, and her grandmother, her only close relative, lived with her son in a two roomed cottage so the girl really had nowhere to go. This thought overcame her fears, and on being given a promise she would never be left in the house on her own again, she decided to stay with the family where she had been very happy.

Each morning and night after this, the family prayers held in the old kitchen asked for protection from Demons. This seemed to do the trick, because the girl was not troubled again for some weeks.

One particular day she stayed in the cowshed after the other milkers had left and was just about to follow them when she heard a voice call, "Nansi, are you afraid of me?"

She tremblingly answered, "Who are you? What do you want?"

The disembodied voice answered, "I am sorry I frightened you the other night, I will not do so again if you do as I say."

She listened while the voice told her to ask her Master if she could place a bowl of bread and milk each night at the foot of the servants' staircase. It had to be the best white bread and the creamiest milk. The girl said she would ask her employer. Her master agreed to the spirit's request, although he was very puzzled.

All went well for some time and the spirit (or *Bwca*, as it was called in Welsh), helped the girl with her work.

Another maidservant called Ellen was intensely curious about the "Bwca" and questioned Nansi frequently about it. She asked, "What did it look like?" and "What did he say?", but the girl refused to answer her. Ellen was rather a spiteful girl and she did not like Nansi, whom she thought far too pretty. She made up a plan to offend the Bwca so that he would blame Nansi and take revenge.

One night after Nansi had placed the nightly offering at the foot of the stairs as usual, the other girl replaced the bread and milk with dirty water from the wool dye. This sent the Bwca mad. He hurled furniture around, spilled the contents of the milk churns in the dairy, and threw the cheeses on the floor. Then he departed, howling with rage, never to return.

Instead, he made his way to another farm and turned his attention to another young servant girl. This girl, whose name

42

was Bronwen, carried out the spirit's request, and all was well for a few months, the spirit doing nearly all her work.

Bronwen was consumed with curiosity to see what the Bwca looked like. She was forever asking him to manifest, but a good humoured low chuckle was the only answer.

One night the farmer's wife, daughter and the maidservants had been spinning. While chatting they compared the whiteness of each others' hands. Suddenly a deep voice said, "My hands are the whitest", and a shapely white hand appeared in the air above their heads. This scared them all except Bronwen, who was a very bold girl. Now she wanted to know his name more than ever.

She pleaded with him but again he refused to answer her request, but did not seem cross with her.

She said "How did you come here?"

"In a jar of barm," was his answer.

Bronwen felt she simply must see the Bwca (who used to spin for her each night), as well as find out his name. One night, after placing his supper at the foot of one staircase, she crept up another into the room used for spinning, and hid. Soon the Bwca came in, seated himself at the wheel, and began spinning. As he spun, he sang alound, "Silly old Bronwen — my name is Garym a Throt." He was completely naked, and had an ugly face with a very long pointed nose. The girl crept away quietly, very pleased with herself.

The next night when Bronwen set out his supper she said, "There you are, Garym a Throt." Something battered her in the face, the farmhouse door shut with a bang, and once more the spirit departed.

At the next farm he became friendly with a farmhand called Huw. He worked hard for Huw and seemed content. They quarrelled only once. Huw doubted the Bwca could plough a field alone. The spirit became furious and beat Huw severely with a broom. They soon became friends again.

All went well again for some time until Huw left to fight in the Battle of Bosworth in 1485 and was killed. This sent the Bwca mad with grief and he started all sorts of mischief of the type associated with poltergeists. Furniture was hurled around, crockery broken, and servants were slapped in the face. The

43

farmer's wife and daughters' arms were black and blue with pinches.

Outside, the mischief was even more dangerous. Threshing flails and sickles were thrown around the stackyard. The cows were milked dry. The worse incident of all was when the spirit harnessed the oxen to a plough and drove them into the river, and they were badly injured by the plough before drowning.

The now terrified household implored the farmer to do something. He finally called in a local wise man to exorcise the Bwca.

After a terrible, exhausting struggle the exorcist managed to make the Bwca manifest itself. The wise man grabbed its long nose and put a small iron bar through it. The Bwca howled and howled. Chanting a further piece of exorcism he commanded the spirit to go to Egypt and enter a spot in the banks of the River Nile and there to stay for a thousand years.

No-one in the district ever saw or heard of the Bwca again.

Distinguished Victorian and Edwardian Researchers argued with each other. Pwca'r Trwyn was named because it was first said to have manifested at Trwyn Farm; other said the Spirit had a long nose — argument agrees better with what the wise man was supposed to have done.

AN OLD MAN REMEMBERS

The elderly man sat contentedly puffing at his pipe while rocking himself gently backwards and forwards in his rocking chair. Then, like all old men, he began to think about the past. Was it really all of seventy years ago that he, Tommy Evans, experienced something supernatural as he made his way home from Llanidloes school, a happy ten year old boy?

He recalled hurrying to call on his grandparents in the hope of a slice of *Bara Brith* (Welsh Currant Bread) such as only *Nain* (Grandmother) could make. As he went, like all children do, he scuffled his feet through the autumn leaves lying untidily all around. The piles of leaves were especially thick near the front gates of an old, almost ruined in parts, mansion and made a lovely scrunch scrunch sound as he walked along. It was then his toe struck something hidden in the leaves. He cleared away some of them, and there lay a curiously shaped bottle, made of glass.

Tommy picked it up and now years later remembered clearly what he saw inside the bottle. It appeared to be a black fly unlike any other he had seen in his young life. It looked very dead, but he did not open the bottle.

He decided to take it to *Taid* (Grandfather), who was the fountain of all wisdom to his ten year old grandson. He would know for sure what kind of a fly it was. Maybe the insect was only sleeping, but having been stung several times by wasps, the boy was taking no chances.

He began to run all the way to his grandparents' tiny cottage, which was made of Welsh stone, the kind that lasts for ever. Too excited at his find to ask for the piece of Bara Brith, Tommy dashed into the house shouting, "Look what I have found", brandishing the bottle.

His grandfather was sitting near the table, just about to have his tea, and he said "Easy now, *bach* (dear), it is breaking the bottle you will be. What is in it?"

"I found it outside the old mansion gates, shall I open it, Taid? It has got such a funny black fly inside it."

Through the years the old man pictured the surprised look on his Taid's face, replaced in an instant by a cautious one.

Tommy said, "Nain, can I have a spoon or something to open this bottle?"

Before his Nain could answer him his Taid shouted sharply, "No, no, leave it alone. Take it back to where you found it. I will come with you and we will bury it there."

Very taken aback by now, Tommy said, "What is the matter, Taid, it is only an old bottle with a dead fly in it. I just wanted to know if you could tell me what sort it is and if the old creature is dead."

"Wait, I have changed my mind, we will call on the Rector and show the bottle to him," said his grandfather.

At this the boy's grandmother said, "Changed your mind, Hugh bach, lost it you mean, boyo. What will the Reverend gentleman think of you bothering him with a silly old thing like that?"

The old man did not answer her but picked up his battered old straw hat, took a walking stick from the corner of the kitchen, and said "Come on Tommy."

Off they went, carrying the bottle carefully, taking turns because Tommy was clamouring to carry it all the way back himself. He chattered incessantly as they went along. "What is wrong with you, Taid? It is only rubbish," he said.

Then he too thought his Taid a little mad, but of course he was very old. Eighty-five his Mam said Taid was.

Fed up with Tommy's chatter, the old man said, "All right, bach, I will tell you a story."

Now the boy was very keen to hear stories of all kinds, but he felt this was not quite the time for Taid to tell one. Oh well, he thought, I might as well listen or he will be vexed. They both sat on a pile of leaves and Tommy, although impatient to reach the Rectory, prepared to listen.

Through the years Tommy heard his Taid telling him in a trembling voice, "The Manor was lived in in the year 1730 (I think that is the right date) by a Lady Jeffereys. Everyone round here knew her, not because she was pretty, and good and kind, but because she was a cruel and wicked woman. She treated all her staff like dogs. The young maid servants were beaten soundly for the least offence, especially her personal maid. If this young girl of fourteen even so much as accidentally pulled one of her ladyship's strands of hair while dressing it, her mistress attacked her fiercely, often blacking her eyes in the process. Farm servants were turned out of their cottages if they dared to ask for the roof or walls to be repaired. It made no matter how many young children they had, out they went, even in deep winter. Lady Jeffereys had full control of everything, since her husband, the Lord of the Manor, had left her a widow in her early twenties. Tenants, servants and even her estate Bailiffs wished her dead and in Hell. They were all terrified of her cruelty."

Tommy remembered how fed up he was getting with his grandfather's tale. What on earth had it to do with the fly in the bottle? He dared not show his impatience because his Taid was quick tempered and might decide not to call on the Rector, but simply bury the bottle with strict instructions to his grandson not to touch it.

Now the old man was coming to the point of the story.

"Lady Jeffereys died before she reached forty years and fairly quickly the mansion and lands began to show the result of neglect. There were no heirs to carry on after her death; not even one relative could be found. About ten years after she had been buried in the vault of the Manor's private chapel her unquiet spirit began to make appearance in the Manor grounds and the village nearby. At times it would manifest as an almost naked beggar in rags, uttering fearful howls, and if any came within range of the apparition, it would advance with fingers stretched out like claws, ready to attack. Only a few brave souls from the village did do so much as attempt to approach the horror, but they soon turned and ran. At other times it would be dressed as a grand Lady with rustling silk clothes and powdered hair. Its jewels would flash in the sunshine or moonlight. This ghost could be seen at any time of the day or night in the locality. At first the hauntings were few and far between but later increased until no-one would go within half a mile of the once magnificent mansion."

By now Tommy was interested about the Ghost, but as his grandfather's tale of horror went on, he became frightened and glanced at the bottle frequently.

"Well, finally, the people of the village went to see the Rector and demanded he exorcise the spirit of Lady Jeffereys," went on his Taid, apparently unaware of the boy's reaction.

"The Rector did his best but failed entirely to send the unquiet spirit back to Hell. It was far too strong for the likes of him. The villagers were angry and demanded that he should call in a very famous exorcist of that time to rid the Parish of the terrifying ghost of her former Ladyship. The Rector agreed to call in this man, and so one moonlit night the exorcism began. Standing outside the Spirit's former home, the exorcist commanded her to appear. He had no close audience, no-one was silly enough to approach, but many gathered at a safe distance and saw what was taking place. When things became too terrifying they moved back quickly, and this happened several times. This very experienced exorcist found he had a real battle on his hands, as the Spirit was determined not to give in. It followed the pattern of all Evil Spirits manifesting in those times, by changing into various animal shapes associated with the Devil. Suddenly it assumed the shape and grand dress of Lady Jeffreys. In this guise it attacked the exorcist again and again, frothing at the mouth as it did so, and extending long nailed hands covered with earth towards him as if it meant to claw his eyes and face."

"Protected by a circle of yew and rowan branches liberally sprinkled with salt which had been blessed by the Rector, the exorcist stood his ground, but exhaustion was taking over. His voice became weak from three hours of chanting. At last he won, and the evil spirit of her Ladyship, without assuming any more animal shapes, suddenly shrank, taking on the form of a small black fly which crawled around outside the exorcist's protective circle, which he had made from yew tree branches. He picked up the insect and put it into a glass bottle, and no-one knew where he had taken it."

"Now Tommy, do you think Lady Jeffereys is in this bottle?"

Tommy remembered how he hastily let go of the bottle and it fell into a pile of leaves. "You take it, Taid," he said in a shaky voice.

His grandfather paused a minute to say a little prayer, then picked up the bottle and the two made their way quickly to the Rectory.

The door was opened by the Rector himself. On hearing their story, he agreed to take charge of the bottle, but no-one ever found out what happened to it afterwards.

Tommy went on puffing his pipe and fell to wondering where his grandfather had heard the story of the wicked Lady Jeffereys.

Had he made it all up? Had the fly been put in the bottle by a boy for a joke, and he and his grandfather been made fools of? He had not made up the story of finding the bottle. An old man himself now, he had heard and seen many things. Could he believe the ghost story? Oh well, there were more things in Heaven and Earth some old play writer had said, long, long ago, he mused.

Tommy laid down his pipe on the little table near him and nodded off to sleep in the manner of the aged.

A RIVERSIDE TRAGEDY

There was a drowning and a suicide in 1705 near the Grove Caves by the River Rheidol, Machynlleth (which is in mid Wales) that spoilt what had once been a pleasant walk.

Right up to the commencement of the twentieth century there were many tales of the area being haunted by frightening ghosts. The origin of this tale is that a shepherd and a dairy maid were in love. One of their favourite walks was close to the Grove Caves. They married and settled down in a tiny stone cottage on the river bank, where they were ideally happy. They eagerly awaited the birth of their first child at the time of the tragedy. The young wife, who was only just sixteen, was getting near her time and her husband was always pleading with her to take good care of herself and stay near home.

One day she had visited the local market with a group of friends. They were young married girls like herself, ex-school companions of hers. In that area the mist, then as now, used to descend quickly in the late autumn afternoons, and that particular day was no exception. The girl tried to keep up with her companions, but found it difficult, as it had been a long tiring, although happy, day. She felt herself getting wearier and wearier and the child seemed extra heavy inside her.

Soon she realised she was lost in the mist. She could hear her friends calling her but her own answers became very faint. Some of her friends turned back but could not find her. There was no response to their shouts. Soon they were all searching with no result.

Before long a large piece of woollen material, obviously from her shawl which appeared to have been caught on a thorn bush, was found. This made the searchers realise the girl must have stumbled in the mist and fallen into the river. Anyone falling into that deep part of the Rheidol would have been swept away and drowned.

Her body was never found, and her young husband went crazy with grief. He ignored all his friends. He was to be seen scouring the countryside, calling her name, day after day. No-one dared approach him too closely, because he had become a dangerous lunatic. He was a danger except to the farmer whose shepherd he

50

had been from when he was about ten years old. He still kept his employment. One morning he failed to collect his employer's sheep from the farm.

The farmer went to his (until then good and faithful) shepherd's cottage. There, across the doorstep, lay the young man's body covered in blood.

He had slit his own throat.

Then began the terrible hauntings.

A spectre of a young woman appeared. It wore a shredded red shawl. Green weeds covered its hair and hung down on to the shoulders. At times its spectral body shone white, then red. Other times the green weeds covered its skeleton-like body.

It was seen firstly by a shepherd. He saw it place a white bundle on the floor. Wailing loudly the apparition went round and around the cottage. Seeing the shepherd approaching, it started throwing stones towards him. All the time blasphemy came from the bony lips. Finally it picked up the luminous bundle and vanished. The man ran off in terror, as did anyone else who came across the horrible phantom from time to time.

Only the spectre of the drowned young woman was ever recorded as being seen. The hauntings by the spirit of the young husband were noisy. Sounds of heavy trampling footsteps and loud screams were sometimes heard. Stones were thrown around the Caves and the cottage by some invisible hands, mostly at the time of the full moon. His spectre never appeared.

Over the years the happenings were rumoured around the area and embellished, as usually occurs in the telling of ghost tales.

The drowning and suicide were true.

THE MYSTERIES OF NANNAU

In the Llanfachreth area which lies above Dolgellau, Merionethshire, North Wales, is the ancient family seat of one of Wales' most prominent family, the Vaughans. Nannau has never had a completely happy history and has its share of ghostly tales through the centuries. The deer of Nannau must always remain on the estate or great disaster will befall the Vaughan family. The old saying is: "There must be deer at Nannau as long as the sun shines and water flows."

The four cross roads cutting across the Llanfachreth-Dolgellau road to the drive of Nannau mansion and the deer park is claimed to have been haunted for at least two centuries up to the present time. The ghost is in the form of a beautiful young lady and it is accompanied always by the phantom of a small dog. In life she became the object of the affection of one of the then Lord Vaughans of Nannau. She refused to have anything to do with him. One day as she was walking her pet dog, he dragged her into the woods in the deer park, seduced and then murdered her. He killed the little dog in case it would lead someone to her grave.

Not very long after he had committed the murder, a game-keeper heard barking late at night from the direction of the kennels behind the mansion. On going to investigate, he said he saw the form of a lady dressed in white walking along the path leading to the deer park. With the form, was the shape of a little dog. He followed the phantom, which crossed a little bridge where it vanished. The man ran back and reported what he had seen to one of the Vaughan family, and servants were ordered to dig close to the bridge. They found the body of the lady and her pet dog. No action was taken against the murderer.

Opposite to Nannau gates is a small well named *Ffynnon y Mulod*, in English "Well of the Mules". It was built by a Sir Robert Williams Vaughan, whose hobby was masonary and mules were used to cart stones. At that time in history all the water for the mansion was carried, and he thought a well for the mules and horses would be convenient.

A very mettlesome stallion had been taken by a groom to drink at the well. Something disturbed the horse and caused it to rear wildly and the groom who was inexperienced failed to bring it under control. The animal brought its two front feet on to the groom's skull, killing him instantly. The legend was that what had caused the horse to rear were daffodils swaying in the breeze, in the April moonlight.

Ever after people in the area used to relate that on a moonlit night in the month of April the sound of the frantic neighing of a horse could be heard together with dreadful sounds of a human being screaming in mortal agony. No phantoms of the groom or the horse have ever materialised.

A grim story centred on Nannau is told in history. It concerns Owain Glyndŵr, immortal hero of many of the Welsh, and Hywel Sele who supported Henry the Fourth. Owain and Hywel were full blood cousins. As Owain was engaged in fighting Henry, the cousins became estranged. The Abbott of nearby Cymmer Abbey reconciled the two and Owain and Hywel promised they would forget the past. Owain agreed to visit Nannau. Before he visited Nannau, Owain Glyndŵr stayed at Llafachreth at *Cae Madoc* (Madoc's Field) a farmhouse owned by Madoc. After making their peace, the cousins went for a stroll intending to shoot a deer.

One account of the tragedy that took place was that Owain was walking in front of Hywel who aimed an arrow at his cousin's back but it missed him. Owain turned round and shot his cousin dead. No one ever saw Hywel Sele again. An accusation was made against Owain Glyndŵr that he had set Nannau on fire so that Hywel Sele would be presumed burned to death without any part of his body left to identify his corpse. This was proved to be untrue many years later, but it has never been proved what happened on that fatal deer stalking.

In Nannau Park was an ancient oak called *Ceubren yr Ellyll* (The Demon's Tree). All the local people said it was the home of several demons who haunted the park at times.

Many years after his disappearance Hywel Sele's skeleton was found in the oak and was buried at Cymmer Abbey.

In July 1813 Sir Richard Colt drew a sketch of the tree. That night it was struck by lightning. Candlesticks were made from the trunk for the mansion, also cups. On her marriage to Lord Snowdon Princess Margaret was presented with a casket made from the oak inscribed "Ceubren yr Ellyll". It has been said that

Hywel Sele's ghost haunts the grounds of Nannau seeking revenge on his cousin.

In early records it is stated that on the Nannau estate is a peak called *Moel Ophrom* (Ophrom's Hill) where the Giant Ophrom used to make his home. On the neighbouring peak called *Cader Idris* (Idris' Chair) lived his friend the Giant Astronomer Idris. During the sixteenth century, the name was said to be Offrwm, which meant sacrifice. This conclusion was reached because on the Nannau estate there was a farm called Boethuog, probably a derivative of *Porth yr Euog* (Gateway of the Guilty) and the Peak was called *Moel Offrwm* (Hill of Sacrifice). Legend said if an intended sacrifice reached the farm they could claim sanctuary and escape being sacrificed.

On the lower part of the southern side of the peak is a field, which was called *Ffridd Cymorth* (Field of Succour). It was very difficult to clamber up the incline but if the victims reached the field, relatives and friends were allowed to assist them to climb to their horrible end. Not a particular comfort that would seem. No one ever recorded why human beings were condemned to sacrifice or by whose decree. There were many tales over many years of terrible screams and pleas for mercy to be heard on moonlit nights at the foot of Moel Offrwm.

In 1964, the deer deserted Nannau deer park and took to the hills. That year a stranger bought the estate from the Vaughans.

THE ST DONAT'S MISER

This quaint ghost story was recorded during the middle of the eighteenth century at St Donat's in Pembrokeshire, South Wales. An old unpopular miser had died without leaving his money to anyone, although people knew he had been wealthy. He did not leave a single penny to his housekeeper. She was a fat, jolly woman who had looked after him for years and deserved better treatment. A month or so after his death, people noticed she looked pale and weary as if she had not slept for nights.

She refused to tell anyone what was wrong with her but finally agreed to tell her friends. She told of how the old miser's ghost haunted her day and night driving her mad with terror. Feeling sorry at the dreadful change in her looks a kind local clergyman offered to hold a service of exorcism at her house and she agreed. Neighbours and friends gathered together for the service, which the clergyman began with a prayer. In the middle of the prayer she screamed, "There he is," pointing across the room. She jumped up out of her chair. "Where have you hidden it? I will do as you say." No one present heard any person speaking to her. Next she went to the wide old chimney breast, put her hand up and drew out a big bag of money.

The room was crowded but she pushed her way through screaming, "Let me go, he will kill me!" and rushed outside.

Some people followed the woman as she ran towards the River Ogmore. The followers suddenly became frightened of seeing the ghost and went back to the service.

They resumed prayer with the clergyman. Shortly afterwards the door crashed open and in stumbled the woman. She was covered with scratches and looked as if she had fallen into the river. She told everyone how the ghost had told her how he hoarded his money which he had stolen and how he could not rest in his grave until the bag containing the money had been thrown into the River Ogmore. The spectre had said he would torment her until she carried out the task of throwing the bag of gold coins downstream. From that night the miser's ghost never appeared to her again.

TWO HORRIBLE APPARITIONS

Nearly three centuries ago near Welshpool, mid Wales, two horrible figures appeared one evening.

A man was taking an evening stroll along the river bank when he saw coming towards him what he first thought was a man. He looked again and the figure seemed to be walking on his hands. It stopped and the man saw to his horror that whatever it was its neck was dangling limply. The thing somersaulted straight into the river. Following behind it a woman was screaming and running. She threw herself into the river.

The spectator could not attempt to rescue the figure as it had obviously been dead before somersaulting into the river as its neck had been dangling. While the man was in shock, the current had carried the woman away.

Later the man learned that close to the place where he had seen the somersaulting figure and the drowning woman a terrible tragedy had taken place. The figure of the somersaulting man had not been a goblin but a phantom who, when he was a man, had committed suicide by severing his throat, and the woman had been his wife who saw him with his neck dangling and drowned herself, afterwards becoming a phantom.

Not more than a mile from where the first nasty incident was alleged to have been seen, on the same night, another happened.

A man was going home by the bright light of the moon when he saw a sight that almost made him insane for life. He had only seen pictures of Goblins or trolls or been given descriptions of those ghastly beings.

Surely this was one of them; it came towards him on all fours, whirling around and around, shaking its massive head from side to side. From its lips came a loud moaning sound. Finally its whirling made it crash into a low stone wall shattering it to bits. The creature stopped shaking its ugly head from side to side, then commenced to whirl again.

The man fell to his knees and prayed for deliverance from such a horror. Immediately after a long wail, the figure rose into the air and vanished. For many months the man suffered from shock and hallucinations and never during the rest of his life went near the place where he had seen the horror.

LLYWELYN EIN LLYW OLAF

When Prince *Dafydd* (David) of Wales died in Aber, near Bangor in 1246, Llywelyn and his brother, *Owain Goch* (Owen the Redhead), the sons of Gruffudd, Dafydd's brother, were created his successors.

Sir Ralph Mortimer, who was married to Prince David's sister, Gwladys, had claimed succession but was rejected by the Welsh.

In 1255, open warfare broke out between the two brothers. Llywelyn easily defeated Owain and imprisoned him in Dolbadarn Castle, a ruin which stands close to Llanberis Lake. Prince Llywelyn swore to drive the English out of Wales and was known as *Llywelyn ein Llyw Olaf* (Our Last Helm).

Llywelyn, stated the old chronicles, had gathered upwards of ten thousand fighting men around him and conquered the whole of North Wales, almost to the gates of Chester. South Wales was also rallying to his banner. King Henry's son, Edward appealed to the Irish for their assistance. Llywelyn, ordered bridges to be destroyed, all fords blocked. He removed his kinsmen and all their women, together with all animals and goods to the mountains of Snowdonia. In 1261, he was joined by Sir Roger Mortimer and his knights and the bitter battles between Wales and England continued. On December 10th in the year 1282 near the scene of a battle at Cilmeri, Builth, Mid Wales, on the banks of the Irfon River, the great hero of the Welsh Nation received wounds from which he was to die the next day. Llywelyn had ordered blacksmiths who were under the command of the senior blacksmith, Madog the Redhead, to reverse the horses' shoes to confuse the enemy as the snow was deep. Llywelyn accompanied by a Squire decided to call at Builth Castle to ask for a few days succour for his men. The treacherous Madog had visited the Castle and betrayed the Prince's ruse.

When the Welsh arrived they were denied entry to the Castle and, on hearing the enemy advancing, scattered in different directions. The Prince rode off accompanied by a squire in order to arrive at the head of his troops.

Both turned into a dingle on the banks of the Irfon and hid in the ditch as they had seen two of the enemy approaching. They were a Norman Knight, Adam de Francton, accompanied by a squire. Francton plunged a dagger into Llywelyn's back then killed the Prince's squire, before galloping away. He thought he had killed both men. The Welsh searched the whole area for their beloved leader but failed to find him.

Adam de Francton hearing Llywelyn was missing, had an intuition and rode back to the dingle. One of the men was dead. The other looked as if he was almost dead but still moving slightly. Near him stood a monk of the Cistercian order who seemed to be preparing to administer, the last rites. The knight had committed his first sin; he flung the monk aside and drove him off with his sword. His second and greatest sin was he hacked off the dying Prince's head. The date was 11th December 1282, ever remembered by fervent Welsh people as one of the nation's blackest days.

Adam de Francton had murdered the man who is recognised by many of the Welsh to-day as the last real prince of Wales by virtue of bloodline.

A triumphant Adam de Francton ordered his men to wrap up the Royal head in branches of broom. During their journey to Conwy Castle where the head was to be presented to Edward the First, it was placed on the ground for fresh broom to replace the bloodstained branches. It was said the shrub, with its beautiful yellow flowers in season, never grew again in those parts of Wales.

When the heartbroken Welsh found the decapitated body of Llywelyn they were horrified to learn Edward would not allow it to be buried in sacred ground anywhere in England or Wales. They made a grave on the banks of the Irfon and placed upon it a memorial stone surrounded by thirteen trees to represent the thirteen counties of Wales. The grave was in a place previously covered with broom but every trace withered never to grow there again. Eventually, by the intervention of Maude de Longspee, Llywelyn's kinswoman, his body was re-interred in the Abbey of Cwm Hir.

I have never seen on record that Llywelyn ein Llyw Olaf ever haunted any particular place in Wales but strange prophecies concerning him made by himself and others seem to have come true. One prophecy tells of how broom would never grow again where his decapitated head would rest on its macabre journey or where his body would lie in an unblessed grave. Another grim one made by an ancient seer to Llywelyn himself was, "My Lord your, crowned head will ride through Cheap."

When Edward received Llywelyn's head from Adam de Francton, it was carried on a lance to the Tower of London to be placed on the highest pinnacle. The head bore a crown made of ivy and was carried on the lance through Cheapside on its shameful journey to the Tower.

Llywelyn's own prophecy was that where even one English soldier crossed the River Irfon at Builth, the river would change its course and grass would grow where the diversion took place. At certain sections of the Irfon this appears to have happened. Adam de Francton learning that Llywelyn had been unarmed, as was his squire, and that by doing so had shamed his own knighthood, became deranged and after dying a dreadful death became a spectre alleged to have been seen by many through the centuries. His tale is told in this book of how he haunted the area of Llantwit.

ST GWYNLLIW AND THE PIRATES

At the beginning of the fifth century there lived in the town of Newport, Gwent, a man aged about thirty, who was said to be the biggest drunkard in the whole area.

He was wealthy and able to buy as much drink as he wanted. His wife, who was a religious woman, used to pray that her husband would give up being nothing but a drunkard and a blasphemer. She also prayed he would become a Christian and wished their children to join with her in asking God to help their Father.

Before long her prayers were answered and she was overjoyed. Her husband was asleep one night after a drunken bout when he heard a voice calling him.

"Foresake your evil ways, turn to me."

The man awoke convinced God had spoken to him. He changed his ways, became baptised a Christian and devoted his wealth to feed the poor. His life was so holy he became called St Gwynlliw.

In acknowledgement to God and to show his love for him, the man vowed to build a fine Church.

He had one problem, where could he build it? There seemed to be no place suitable, until one night St Gwynlliw was visited in his sleep by an Angel. The Angel said, "Search until you find a white ox, pure white except for a black spot on its forehead. Where you find the animal, there you will build your Church." St Gwynlliw found the white ox standing at the top of Stow Hill, Newport. Straight away he built the Church which he named St Woolos. When the Church was finished, St Gwynlliw put a curse on anyone desecrating the Church or stealing anything from it.

Not long after building St Woolos, St Gwynlliw died in the last year of the Fifth century.

About a year after St Gwynlliw's death, pirates sailed up the River Usk. They anchored where the Alexandria Dock, Newport, was constructed centuries later.

As they sailed towards Newport they saw the magnificent Church on the hill and agreed it would be well worth robbing.

After dark, they set off and before long, entered the Church. Their eyes glistened on seeing the massive golden cross encrusted with precious jewels. There was an abundance of jewelled chalices and other Church vessels. They reached their brig safely with their booty, setting sail quickly, unseen.

The waters were calm and all went well until they reached the start of the Bristol Channel. Suddenly, a great wind came out of the sea and clouds raced in the sky, the sea became a boiling mass. Out of the storm, riding the wind, and just above their heads came the figure of a monk flying with arms outstretched. It was St Gwynlliw's spirit carrying out his own curse. He swooped down on to the terrified pirates' deck and scooped up the stolen treasure, flying off with it in his arms — a miracle because it was so bulky and heavy. As he left, the vessel was tossed about from side to side amidst screams from the pirates. She sank to the bottom of the channel within minutes. Every pirate was drowned and the next morning their bodies were to be seen floating on the River Usk.

Renovated first in Norman times, St Woolos still stands in perfection. The only thing that happened to it after the pirates had committed sacrilige, was that one of Oliver Cromwell's troops shot the head off a statue standing in a niche in a tower. This headless statue can still be seen.

PHANTOMS OF THE GLEN

A charming glen close to the little town of Corwen, North Wales looks so peaceful and green that it is hard to associate it with horror.

From the 18th Century onwards it has been known as the scene of violence and of subsequent hauntings.

In the centre of the glen is a stream crossed by a bridge named Pont-y-Glyn. Strolling alongside this stream it comes as a surprise to see it change into a torrent of water at one point and pass through a deep ravine. The visitor has by now walked to a part of this lovely area which has been the subject of ghost stories through Georgian, Victorian and even modern times.

One summer day in 1890 just before the day merged into twilight, a beautiful young servant girl, Betsy, was murdered by a jealous farm servant whose proposal of marriage she refused.

Betsy was employed as a dairy maid in a farm close to Pont-y-Glyn called Garthmeilio. She was madly in love with a young farm servant called Huw who worked on a neighbouring farm. Pont-y-Glyn was their trysting place and on that summer day she had sat on a heap of stones near the stream to eagerly wait her lover's arrival. While she sat looking at the beautiful red sky promising fine weather for the next day and dreaming of Huw, she was unaware of the unsuccessful suitor watching her from a place in the long grass. Before long he drew himself up from his hiding place and tiptoed towards the girl. As he put out his hand to touch her she sprang up from the heap of stones and asked him what he wanted. "You must go away at once because my beloved Huw will be here in a few minutes," she warned. For answer, the man put his large hands around the girl's throat and strangled her within minutes before she had time to cry out.

The tall Welsh hat she had been wearing fell off as he picked up her frail body and slung it over his shoulders. He carried the body to the ravine and threw it into its murky depths.

When Huw, full of happiness at meeting Betsy, came along, he found the Welsh hat lying on the ground but his intended bride was never found.

Everyone concluded she had been murdered, but her murderer was never discovered.

Very shortly after Betsy's disappearance, a ghost appeared in the dairy at Garthmeilio, and from the description of those who said they had seen the spectre, it seemed to be that of the missing girl.

Her broken hearted lover searched month after month for whoever had murdered Betsy, but without success.

As the months went by Garthmeilio no longer appeared to be haunted, but a much more terrifying ghost made its appearance where the Welsh hat had been found. This was described by a farm bailiff who was employed at another farm called Garthbeibio at Llangwm, a tiny hamlet about two miles from Pont-y-Glyn.

He was on his way back from seeing a friend and his route passed near Pont-y-Glyn. The pile of stones near the bridge was still there and sitting on it he said he saw the figure of a young girl dressed in Welsh costume. At first he was not afraid but what happened a few minutes after he had first seen the figure terrified him and remained in his memory forever. The shape of what he took to be a girl started to take on a massive size. The apparition grew larger and larger and filled the whole of the road leading to the bridge. Without waiting to see what would happen next the man ran away from the scene as fast as he could.

Betsy's murder was not the only one in the area; there were many more around this place, the bodies of the victims ending up in the dark ravine. It had become a place of demons and malignant phantoms.

One particularly frightening phantom which everyone said must have been a demon took on a most unexpected shape. It became a massive turkey whose body seemed to be covered with translucent feathers. The bird would fan out its tail and then twirl around madly and like the other phantom it would begin to increase in size. No-one who saw the sight ever stayed to find out how big the turkey would eventually become before disappearing. There was also supposed to be a phantom witch: the ugliest creature imaginable. It appeared to have only one eye in the centre of its face, large fang-like teeth, arms like sticks, ending in claws. It approached the traveller passing through this glen, wailing and making as if to embrance the person by means of its claw-like hands. After confronting the terrified man or woman it sailed up into the air over a clump of trees which formed a wind-break.

Periodically through these trees, a red light would be seen glowing and sometimes moving in and out them. In this glen, which could well be the most haunted in North Wales, there came reports now and again of headless phantom horses being driven by a figure resembling Satan who drove the wildly galloping herd of horses into the ravine at Pont-y-Glyn. Even to this day the area is not one that local people care to walk in after dark, possibly remembering the tales concerning it told by their grandfathers and great-grandfathers.

WELSH DEATH OMENS

This is a gloomy story and if you do not want to feel particularly creepy, do not read it, but I feel sure you will.

The omens are, in order of priority, as follows.

Firstly, the Tolaeth, which covers sounds of knocking, tapping or rapping, or even the sound of footsteps. In one house in Porthcawl, South Wales, there was the sound of footsteps, as if several people were walking up the path leading to the front of the house. This was heard by a married couple in the house and made them feel uneasy. They sat hand in hand and did not speak and before long went to bed. Then came the sound of a door opening and closing. Next came the sound of someone moving chairs. They trembled in their bed and cuddled close. There seemed to be people in the kitchen and there was the sound of something heavy being banged down on the kitchen table. Soon the sounds ceased and all was still. The morning could not come soon enough, and when it did, husband and wife crept downstairs, dreading what they might see, but there was nothing strange in sight, or anything disturbed. The husband went to work, returning at night. The unnatural sound they had heard were on their minds and they were filled with foreboding.

A few more days went by and their minds became easier. They even began to believe they had only imagined the occurrence. They had been tired, the fire had been hot, they might have dozed and were half asleep. The folk in the next cottage might have been moving furniture around although it was late and they were not usually inconsiderate. Life had to go on.

A knock came on the door.

It was a man to tell them their only son had been drowned three days previously. His body was brought home on a plank covered by a blanket, carried up the front path and placed on the kitchen table.

Next is the *Cyhyraeth* (the wailing). A moaning, high or low, is heard, outside a house or moving through a street. If the pitiful moaning is heard resounding along the street, it means a few will die in an epidemic. Sometimes a person's relative hears the wailing, denoting the impending death of the relative or a dear friend. If the cyhyraeth is heard near the sea it means a fatal shipwreck.

While out with her husband one woman heard a sad moaning and wailing. Next morning her husband was brought home dead after an accident in a mine where he had been on night shift. He had not heard the wailing while he was out with his wife on a stroll before getting ready for night shift.

A man was having his usual pint at his local Inn when he heard a curious wailing. He drew the attention of the landlord to it, but he said he had heard nothing.

"Strange," he said, "Now you mention it, my wife said last night she hears a sad moaning noise. I told her it was just the breeze getting stronger."

The man who had been at the Inn told his neighbour's wife of the strange noise.

"Funny, I heard it too last night when I was passing the Inn." She went on to say that it was the cyhyraeth, and someone belonging to the Inn would surely die. As the wife had heard it too, it would not be she who would die.

Next day the villagers heard the landlord had dropped dead the previous night.

In direct contrast to what the woman said, sick people sometimes heard the moaning and died. In one case visitors to the sickroom heard the noise.

One young woman asked her sick father, "Are you worse, I heard you moaning?"

"I did not moan, but it was the cyhyraeth you heard. I will die tomorrow," he replied, and he did.

The sighting of a corpse candle is a dreaded omen. This is a small bluish light, moving like a Will of the Wisp with a slow hovering. It is larger for an adult than a child. It stops outside any house where a person is going to die in the night. It sometimes follows the route from a house to the cemetery where the corpse is to be buried. It is led by the spectral form of the person who is about to die.

Phantom funerals were not such a frequent omen.

The *Deryn Corff* (the corpse bird) very seldom appears. "It is very large and black," some used to say; others, "It is a small brown bird." Another version is a medium-sized bird with no feathers or wings. In each case at night it perches on a wall or roof of a house where someone is to die that night. Also it is agreed that it sometimes calls loudly, *"Dewch, Dewch"* (Come, Come).

Different from the Welsh Hell Hounds, always black, who are omens of death and/or tragedies, the Dog of Death is always white or near white. This dog stands outside a sick person's house and often howls horribly. At other times it crouches in a gateway with a piteous expression on its face.

The old people said they could smell approaching death in a house when they smelled earth. Some said the smell of the flower of the yarrow was a sure sign, even if they were none in the house. It was never allowed inside the house at any time as it was certain to bring death with it.

In Llantwit Major a bell tolling by itself at night foretold the death of one or more residents before morning. Also some said the sound of digging and bumping noises are sometimes heard late at night in a churchyard where St Iltutus is said to be buried. This means a prominent member of the community will die within three days.

CRAIG-Y-NOS

In the lovely Vale of Glamorgan stands the Castle of Craig-y-Nos, once the home of Adelina Patti, the singer of immortal fame.

Long before her time it was said that the Fair Family (*Tylwyth Teg*) kept a vast hoard of their treasure under the Castle in some sort of tunnel or cave.

To reach the Castle they scaled the wall by means of a ladder of pure gold with twenty rungs. (Twenty was a magical number in mythology.) When they had reached the courtyard of the Castle, they came up beside the entrance to the cave which was topped by a massive stone slab. It needed a password for the slab to move and let them in and a different one to let them out again.

For a long time a young shepherd watched the tiny folk carry sacks into the Castle and then return without them. By constant listening the shepherd learned the password used to get into the cave.

One day about noon he decided to try to get into the Castle. Using the magic password he succeeded in getting into the treasure trove room. Suddenly, to his horror, he remembered he had no idea of the password for getting out. In his excitement in watching the comings and goings he had not thought about this. In despair he crouched down in a corner. It was dark when the Fairies came to their cave with some treasure. The fluttering of their candle flames told them someone was there. They soon discovered the intruder, and captured him. They kept him prisoner for seven years before he managed to escape.

During his stay he had learned both passwords. Soon after his escape he told his friend, a local farmer, all about the treasure and the passwords.

The farmer promised to give the shepherd some of the treasure, and set off to find it. The shepherd was too scared to go with him. The farmer managed to get in and out of the cave several times and carry away some treasure, but became greedy and went once too often. One night the Fairy Folk caught him. They were so angry that instead of making him a prisoner like the shepherd, they murdered him, slowly and agonisingly, in spite of his pleas for mercy.

His remains were quartered and hung up on hooks in a room below the Castle. They gave the same treatment to other potential thieves of their treasure.

Many of the older folk in the Craig-y-Nos area say the Castle is haunted by the ghost of the greedy farmer. On quiet nights he is supposed to rattle the iron hooks on which his body had hung until it rotted away. The others who were murdered rattle their hooks and moan, but the farmer's voice is heard above the others crying pitifully, "Let me live, let me live."

When the farmer failed to return home an extensive search was carried out by his friends, but no-one ever knew what had happened to him until one day some ten years after he had vanished.

The shepherd who originally found the cave with all the treasure in it through the years became braver and again started to spy on the Fairy Folk. One moonlight night he saw several of them sitting in a circle talking. They were discussing what they had done to the farmer and their other visitors. When he got home he found he had lost his fear of the Fairy Folk and began to tell everyone about his own experience, and what had been done to the farmer and the others. No-one believed him and they laughed at his imagination.

He told the Vicar of the Parish and even he did not believe him. The shepherd's brain began to be affected and he eventually threw himself into a river and was drowned.

Craig-y-Nos is now up for sale but few people are able to repeat the macabre story of Craig-y-Nos.

Adelina Patti bought the Castle and restored it as the acme of luxury to please her Italian musician husband. None of the builders carrying out the restoration found any trace of bodies or even iron rings suspended from ceilings in rooms underneath the Castle.

It is a very hard item of folklore to credit, even for those who do believe in the Fairy Folk of Wales, the Irish Lephrechauns, or ghosts in general. It might be that the fairy story was made up to cover up thieving by someone in the area who had been caught and then murdered by one of the Castle servants.

THE SNAKES

The absence of vipers in Ireland was compensated for by their abundance in Wales, in particular North Wales. They were in Wales called *Wiberod*, and ranged from simply venomous ones to magic reptiles with wings who were classed as servants of the Devil. Some ancient chroniclers wrote that his Satanic Majesty at times turned himself into a massive snake, suddenly emerging from the undergrowth.

I have read that Victorian historians wrote that wherever there were vipers there were dragonflies nearby whose mission was to be on the watch for snakes. They were called in Welsh *Gwas y Neidr* (Snake Servants). My grandmother once told me of this and she used to warn me to stay away from dragonflies.

Near Llanidloes in mid-Wales a viper made part of the Severn turn bright green where it ran through a nearby wood. The ancients burned down the wood and for a few years nothing more was seen of the viper. It returned and killed two oxen. Gorged with its Gargantuan meal, the viper fell fast asleep. A fisherman crept up to it and killed it by cutting off its head. The creature's blood filled a nearby field which was ever after called *Dolgoch* (the red field).

In Gwibernant, Penmachno, Caernarfonshire, a water snake was greatly feared. It had lived there for centuries, hence the name of *Gwibernant* (direct translation — stream of the snake).

In nearby Hiraethog an outlaw decided to kill the viper but not knowing how to kill it, consulted a local wise man. The outlaw asked the man how he (the outlaw) would die, expecting him to say "snake bite". His answer was, "Of a viper's bite, breaking your neck, and by drowning."

"What a stupid answer — one death is sufficient," said the man.

"But true," was the wise man's answer.

Off went the outlaw to tackle the snake.

It bit him and he fell over a rock, breaking his neck. The impact tossed him into a deep stream beneath a rock. So the prophecy was fulfilled.

His friend, another outlaw, killed the snake, but while fighting it he was uninjured.

On Nannau estate lived a viper called *Gwiber Coed-y-Moch* (The Pigs' Wood Snake). The wood was full of oak trees and the wild and the domestic pigs bred at Nannau loved the acorns in it.

The viper could hypnotise any living thing and then kill it. This power caused the death of pigs, deer, sheep and cattle on the estate, which meant great expense for the owners of Nannau estate, the Vaughans. The Lord of Nannau at that time offered a reward of several heads of cattle to anyone who would kill it.

A shepherd employee of the Vaughans borrowed a large axe from the monks of Cymmer Abbey and killed the troublesome creature. It was buried close to Lake Cynwych at Llanfachreth, which was on the Nannau estate. The inhabitants piled stones on the dead viper's grave, just in case it came alive. The cairn was called *Carnedd y Wiber* (Cairn of the Viper).

Gwion Bach, possibly the son of the first Welsh witch Ceridwen, (but this has never been confirmed), killed a viper at *Llwyn Gwion* (Gwion's Wood) at Ardudwy, not far from Barmouth.

The next day another viper killed Gwion, who had walked a few miles from where he killed the first viper. It drapped his body to where he had killed its companion and laid his body next to the viper's.

Gwion is recorded to have died in different ways and localities.

The heir to an estate named Penhesican in Anglesey was said by a magician to be destined to be killed by a viper's bite. For safety his father sent the boy to be educated in England.

A huge viper came to live on the estate and the squire offered a substantial reward for its death. The servants dug a pit and placed a brass dish at the bottom. The viper went to look at the shining object and fell into the pit, where it was easily killed.

The squire sent for his son as the viper could no longer harm him. After arriving home the young man asked to see the viper's carcase. Reluctantly, his father ordered the carcase of the creature to be dug up. This was done and father and son went into the pit. The carcase had not decayed but lay curled up, looking natural.

The son said, "Evil creature, you have kept me from home for years." He kicked it and one of its fangs pierced his boot and the poison from it killed him instantly.

In one ancient tale the viper has been described as a dragon. There were no records of dragons being in existence in Wales at that time in the fifteenth century. Some people said the dragons were flying snakes.

The saints of Wales are recorded as having killed snakes.

The life of a man who was bitten by a viper in Clwyd, North Wales, was saved by the prayers of St Gwasibardig, who also prayed there might be no more snakes in that county evermore. His prayers do not seem to have worked very well (except to save the man's life).

One woodland at Loggerheads, on the main Ruthin to Mold road, has always abounded with snakes. Legend said every Midsummer Eve hundreds met there to hold a sort of celebration. The flying serpents were represented in force.

Until about two years ago notices were posted up at the entrance to Loggerheads Woods, "Beware of Adders". Since Loggerheads, once a long distance Bus Stop Café, has been turned into a small pleasure park. The snakes have departed in the main, but in the summer of 1989 a few adders and grass snakes have been seen in the area.

There is an account of a huge viper scared of St Samson eating itself up alive. It started the grisly operation from its tail up. This was several hundreds of years ago. St Carannog had a pet viper which followed him everywhere in Mid-Wales. It was recorded at about the same period. St Keneldon, daughter of St Brychan, while crossing the Severn had to pass a large gathering of vipers, who hissed and made to attack her, making a circle around her. She fell on her knees and prayed, and every viper was turned into a stone for many miles.

One famous tale of a flying viper comes from Clwyd. It tells of how Denbigh acquired its name. A flying viper called a Bych killed many people in that area of Clwyd. This was in the time of Sir John Salisbury, nicknamed *Sion y Bodiau* (John of the two thumbs) as he had two thumbs on each hand. He was at one time married to Catrin Tudor of Berain, Queen Elizabeth the First's cousin. He fought the viper and killed it. Triumphantly he shouted, *"Dim Bych"* (no Bych). He held up his hand saying in Welsh (With my white hand I killed it [*a'm llaw weni*], so he called his home "Lleweni". The town was named Denbigh.

As described in the account of Loggerheads in Clwyd, the

midsummer snake gatherings were held all over Wales. At these gatherings "snake stones" were made. In Mid and South Wales during the gatherings this strange phenomenon was recorded as happening the most frequently. Forming a circle the snakes hissed and a bubble came from their mouths. This bubble was spat out and formed a glass ring. They were called *Gleiniau Nadroedd*. Anyone finding one was supposed to be very lucky and would always prosper.

The best description of a flying serpent was recorded in the year 1639. A blacksmith, Owen ap Harri Dafydd, said he saw a flying snake in Llanfair Isgaer, near Caernarfon. It had a very long body, covered in shiny green scales, short wings, and it glared at Owen with glowing red eyes. He said he was drunk at the time or he would never have had the courage to attack it. With his stout stick he beat it to death. The whole event could have been put down to the man's drunken imagination, except for the fact the creature's body was found next day. It was lying at the foot of a monument in the centre of Llanfair Isgaer.

In the Vale of Edeyrnion in a grove near Plas y Faerdref in 1812, a flying snake just like the one Owen ap Harri described was seen while it was flying low, to snatch up lambs and swallow them while it was in flight. A hunt was organised and the creature was seen on the ground. When it saw its would-be killers approaching it turned into a huge bird and flew off.

THE SKULL OF FFANGALLT —
VERSION ONE

About four miles from Holywell, near Rhes-y-Cae, a district full of supernatural legend, a Manor once stood on the site of the present Ffangallt Farm. It was a motte built by a Norman Baron at the start of the twelfth century and was made of wood and clay.

Within its Great Hall was a macabre object in a golden casket. It was the skull of Prince Dafydd of North Wales, kinsman by marriage of Henry I. He was murdered with his twin brother.

There are remains of the skull at the farm to this day. It stands on a mantle shelf inside a glass cabinet which was made for it a century ago. In those days the casket stood on a stone slab in the Great Hall of the Manor and was treated with respect and guarded well. This was because of a prophecy that if the casket and its contents left the Manor, great misfortune would fall upon the Baron and his family, including death by accident or murder.

Without any apparent reason a run of bad luck came upon the Baron's family. His heir was out hunting when an arrow pierced him to the heart, killing him instantly. Next, the eldest daughter of the family fell into a swamp near the Manor and was sucked in to her death. Money became scarce, the crops failed, and despair descended on the once happy home.

One day, the Lady of the Manor noticed the casket was not in the Hall. Frantically everyone searched in vain, and a Wise Man from Holywell was called to the Manor because the misfortunes were thought to be connected with the skull's disappearance.

He interviewed the servants first; one particular man seemed more scared than the others. The wise man stared hard at this servant, who suddenly screamed, "Oh, Jesu, have mercy, it is above my head." Everyone looked up and there, floating in mid air was a skull. Only the brave stayed where they were; the rest ran out in terror. The Wise Man said to the servant, "Tell me what you did and the skull will not trouble you again."

The man said he had not heard what was in the casket. He stole it and took it to one of the farm's outhouses to see whether there were jewels in it that he could sell. When he prised it open, he found the skull and dropped it in terror. After a while he plucked up enough courage to take the skull to the Churchyard and bury it. He left the casket in the outbuildings. Soon after this, one night he heard a terrible wailing noise, then a loud knock. He opened the door of his bed-chamber and outside, about ten feet in the air was suspended the skull, grinning horribly. The servant was petrified but could not tell anyone of what he had done, as the Baron would have him killed. For a month he saw the skull several times, and then someone told him how there was a curse upon the family of the Manor because the skull was missing.

The Wise Man said, "The Baron will not have you put to death, he will only be too glad to have the curse lifted."

Quickly the man led him to where he had left the empty casket. The Wise Man carried it to the Churchyard accompanied by the servant, who showed him where he had buried the skull.

After digging it up the Wise Man said, "Hold the casket." Trembling, the man obeyed but nearly dropped it because when the Wise Man placed the skull gently into its casket, its bony jaws opened and the skull gave a long sigh. In a few minutes the casket was back in the Great Hall, and peace and prosperity returned gradually to the Manor. No-one knew what happened to the servant, as he disappeared the day after the return of the skull.

Some ten years ago at the time I visited the farm the skull was known in the household as 'Dafydd'. Members of the family were not keen on visitors calling to see it just in case Dafydd came disturbed.

The farmer's wife told me she had seen another report of a servant girl having a row with the farmer's wife and throwing the casket into a pond near the farm for revenge.

Historians prefer the manservant theory. I do not; the version I prefer is included in this book.

THE SKULL OF FFANGALLT — VERSION TWO

This is another version of the tale of the Ffangallt skull, which starts with some history relating to Ffangallt Manor.

The Lord of the Manor sent a message to his Lady that a guest was coming that day. He did not tell her it was her kinsman, of whom she was very fond, Prince Dafydd of Wales, son of Owain Gwynedd. Dafydd was fleeing from the English, who had offered gold for his head.

On this day she was just thinking about him and of his past glories and of how the Welsh bards praised him. Suddenly, she started out of her reverie as a horn sounded outside the Manor Gates. It was her husband arriving with his guest. As she went forward to greet them she was delighted to see it was Prince Dafydd. Her husband walked into the stately hall side by side with his guest. A poet says they were in marked contrast to each other: the Prince so tall and handsome, his curly black hair touched with silver, his host sallow-complexioned and surly-looking.

The Baron's wife greeted Dafydd with affection. They sat to commence the banquet and many toasts were drunk. Laughter rang through the hall and all seemed merry. A few knights thought the Prince, who had looked so happy, suddenly began to look ill.

He stood up and looked at the Lord of the Manor, on whose face was a gloating smile. Prince Dafydd spoke and his words struck horror to the company. He said that he knew he had been betrayed. Poison had been put into his cup. He went on to say he knew his head would bring gold to his murderer, gold which his host would rush to claim before his body was cold. Turning to the Lady of the Manor he begged her to see that his remains had a decent burial. Referring to his head he said part of him would be away from the Manor and evil would befall all the guilty present. No harm would come to his kinswoman or her son at any time. He delivered a curse that until the missing part of him crossed the threshold of the Manor and remained inside it for ever, he would haunt the place. Ill luck would fall on the Baron and his house.

The Lady screamed as Prince Dafydd fell dead, and she vowed

she would leave the Manor next day to spend the rest of her life in a convent. She carried out her word, but before she left she ordered her servants to bury the prince's body in holy ground. Her son she took with her to live in cloisters, putting him in the protection of the church.

Her wicked Lord cut off his victim's head and rode to Chester with it. At Chester it was put on a pole at the city gate. He received a quantity of gold in exchange for the Welsh hero's head. Only two of his knights accompanied the murderer to Chester. The remainder of his knights saw to the burial of the prince in a nearby Abbey.

Disaster after disaster fell on the Manor and its occupants. One day the Baron was in retreat from an encounter with another knight and raced his charger for home. As he neared his manor he was attacked and trampled to death by wild cattle.

Prince Dafydd's kinswoman's son inherited the manor and its lands. He went to Chester before going to live in the manor, to claim Prince Dafydd's skull from Chester Gates. Surrounded by praying knights and monks he took down the skull and reverently took it home. It was placed on a pall covered with purple velvet. When they reached the manor he lead a procession of priests and knights into the hall and placed the skull in a special place there. A prayer was said for the repose of Prince Dafydd's soul and for the new baron and his family. It was then announced that so long as the skull remained there until it crumbled into dust there would be no curse unless anyone dared to remove it.

Hundreds of years, in fact over six hundred passed. The manor fell into ruins and a farm was built on the site. There is still a farm there, incorporating some parts of the original manor building into the farmhouse. There is a legend that if anyone digs for gold or treasure on the land that used to surround the old manor, things begin to happen. Torrential rain falls amid storms of thunder and lightning. There have been tales years ago of winds of hurricane proportions arising as soon as a treasure seeker commenced digging. Some have, in spite of the sudden change in climate as they started to dig, carried on, unearthing burial urns, some gold and silver coins, and bones. It has been many years since anyone has found anything on the land.

In early Georgian days the skull vanished for a time. A maid at the farm hated the skull, which had been placed on top of a tall bookcase. Her very particular and severe mistress insisted the servants kept the place spotless and shining. One day she told the girl to dust the bookcase. The girl already knew she was not to dust the skull. When the girl had finished the mistress took a book down and found it covered with dust. She took several down and dust flew everywhere. She sent for the girl and threatened her with dire punishment if she found any dust on the books again. "Clean it before you go to bed," she shouted. The girl was covered with dust and cried, "It is that nasty old bone, but I am not allowed to dust it." She wept.

From time to time her mistress shook books and always dust flew around. Soon the girl began to think there was a spiteful spirit that lived in the skull which threw the dust about. One day she climbed up high on to the bookcase. Covered with dust she carried the skull carefully out and without anyone seeing her, flung it into the farmyard pond. No-one noticed the absence of the skull as it had been hardly visible because the bookcase was so tall.

The servant girl did not look well but she said there was nothing wrong with her.

Two days after throwing the skull there was a dreadful shriek in the middle of the night. The male occupants of the house ran outside. The farmer's wife thought she recognised the girl's voice, and not finding her in bed, followed. It was a dark and foggy moonless night. They heard a splashing from the pond and moaning and made their way towards the pond. A female figure in white came out of the pond screaming, "The dead man's curse is on me!" She clutched the skull to her and would not let anyone touch it until she reached the bookcase. She asked the men to lift her so she could put the skull back in its place.

She then fell in a fit. When she came to they found she was paralysed. For months she lay a helpless invalid until even the doctor agreed she was cursed. Slowly she recovered, but a few times she stumblingly made her way to the pond and waded into it. Then she bent and searched in the water. Some of the servants followed her but did not disturb her, just waited for her to return to the house. She never smiled or laughed again and her sleep was disturbed by nightmares of the skull. She spent a great deal of time crying. Never did she allow anyone to mock at the skull but used to go close to the bookcase and say, so an ancient poet says, "Beware, ye thoughtless ones reverence the dead."

It might be thought that under the circumstances she would eventually drown herself, but the poet does not say what happened to her, neither is there any record.

THE MERCIFUL SISTER

The west border of the village of St Athan, Glamorganshire, South Wales, was once the site of two castles in close proximity, the "West Orchard Castle" and the "East Orchard Castle". They protected the orchards which were said to be the finest in Britain. Both were erected by a Norman Knight, Rogerus de Berkerolles, who accompanied William the Conqueror to England. In the thirteenth century both castles were destroyed by a fierce Welsh chieftain, Ifor Bach.

People used to say two ghosts haunted the West Orchard. One person said she had felt one of the phantoms pull at her skirt as if to attract her attention. Those who claimed to have seen the ghosts said that one of them only appeared in the very early morning in the month of June throughout the centuries.

In life the phantoms were two loving sisters. Sir Humphrey de Berkerolles who had inherited the wealth of the family had married a very young and lovely young girl. Her name was Joyce, but most of the inhabitants of the area said she was called Tybote. That seemed a more Norman name than Joyce.

Archbishop Baldwin in 1188 preached on behalf of the Crusades in Wales, which resulted in many Knights becoming Crusaders. Sir Humphrey was one, much to the grief of his young wife, who begged him not to leave her. He told her his Christian duty came first. Sir Humphrey survived and returned to St Athan to the great joy of his wife.

A Norman Knight who had tried in vain in Sir Humphrey's absence to seduce her, in revenge at her rejection, said she had been unfaithful with him while Sir Humphrey was away, not once but many times, and also with other men. Sir Humphrey was furious to the point of madness and would not believe her denial of unfaithfulness. He locked her up in West Orchard Castle and warned anyone on pain of instant death not to give her any food or water. In their charity several people employed in the castle did feed her.

When Sir Humphrey found out he devised a cruel death for his innocent wife. He had her hands tied to her sides and made sure her feet were tied together. She was then buried up to her neck in earth in a location close to the West Castle. Sir Humphrey made one concession — her sister could visit her once each day in the morning.

Her sorrowing sister made the journey at dawn each day while the dew was thick on the grass. She wore a long silk gown, which trailed through the grass, gathering the dew. She then walked backwards and forwards, brushing her sister's lovely face with the dew. She told the suffering young wife she and everyone knew she was blameless. For ten days the sister carried out her mission of mercy, but when she went on the eleventh day, she found Lady Tybote had died from the torture during the night. Just before dying she whispered her love for her husband, absolving him of his sin of murder. The murdering husband, who had formerly been religious, became a violent drunkard and blasphemer.

About a year after the young wife's death, a Knight told Sir Humphrey on oath that she had been utterly faithful to him. He went mad and had to be imprisoned in the West Orchard Castle by his brother. He used to rave and scream about the wrong he had done. His pleas for his beautiful and faithful wife to return to him rang through the castle. He died after a few years, a raving lunatic, still screaming her name.

The ghost of the loving sister was reported to be seen re-enacting her daily errand of mercy, trailing the hem of her gown in the dew. Some folk said pitiful pleading for mercy could be heard on a still night which could only have come from the phantom lips of the wronged young wife who died in agony.

Her ghost has also been reported seen as well as heard at various times through the centuries. It materialises as a young, tall, lovely young woman, wandering around the outside walls of West Orchard Castle at intervals in the evenings during all seasons. Wearing a long white dress it stands on the spot where the husband had his wife buried alive for adultery she did not commit. Slowly, slowly it sinks into the earth. It was strange this phenomenon was only seen at night, in contrast to the ghost of the sister, which only appeared at or around dawn during the months of June and July.

It has never been reported that the ghost of the murdering husband has been seen. To anyone studying ghost lore this is rather unusual, as murderers' ghosts usually materialise in remorse; and he had plenty to answer for.

LIGHTNING STRIKES

An old saying, "lightning does not strike in the same place twice," does not apply to a house in the Llanarmon District of Clwyd. Where this house stands there used to be at the start of the last century a farmhouse occupied by two farmers, who were twin brothers, called Eifion and Harri Griffiths.

They were known in the locality as villains of the worst kind, and were shunned by most of the villagers of Llanarmon. There was no wicked deed they would not stoop to if it meant that it was a source of money, jewels or land. Some owners of a few acres of land in the locality had been cheated of them by the brothers, who eventually became two of the biggest land owners for miles around. Villagers spoke in whispers of the murders the brothers were supposed to have committed. Whether these rumours were true or not, neither brother was brought to trial for either theft or murder. It seemed as if everyone was terrified of speaking out against them for fear of their vengeance.

A short distance from where the brothers farmed was a small cottage where an old woman had lived by herself for many years. She was a respectable old woman, a faithful church-goer and was supposed to have a great deal of money in the house, as well as valuable jewellery, which she would undoubtedly leave to the Church. She had been born of a wealthy family in the district and was the last of her line.

The two brothers knew all about her and one dark night they forced their way into her cottage. In spite of her pleading they knocked her unconscious, stole her possessions, and set the cottage on fire. It was made of more wood than stone and had a thatched roof, so it burned quickly to the ground. There was no-one to accuse them of this murder and arson, although one or two people had their suspicions, which they dared not voice.

In those superstitious days, the brothers were reputed to have dealings with the Devil. There was an account of the two men having been seen in the company of Satan, given by more than one person. A not very bright member of the community, a youth of about sixteen swore that he was returning from work from a farm on the Black Mountain just behind the village of Llanarmon when he noticed a red glow at the edge of a small wood. He was extremely curious and went to investigate, but what he saw made him run away in abject terror.

After he had reached his home and could speak coherently, he told a strange tale of what he had seen. He said that when he got nearer to the glow he could see clearly three figures and one of them could be no other than Satan. The youth said he could identify Satan by his shape and long swishing forked tail and the red glow around his body. The three, with hands joined, walked slowly in a circle. He was not sure who the two men were and he was so scared he had not stayed long enough to find out. People who listened to his story were sure they had been Eifion and Harri communing with Satan.

Some time went by and the brothers seemed to amass even more money and land than they already had.

One stormy January night the sound of thunder echoed around the farmhouse. Streaks of lightning ran up and down the sides of the Black Mountain at the rear of the farm. The brothers were sitting cosily by their kitchen fire supping ale when a shaft of lightning struck the chimney of the house. It came down the chimney, split the chimney breast open and struck Eifion, killing him instantly.

Now Harri was more wicked than ever, but he did not miss Eifion much. The roof was repaired and a new chimney breast built.

One hot July day, six months after Eifion's death, Harri was in the kitchen. A storm came up and lightning struck the roof of the farmhouse once more. Suddenly the whole house became alight; and Harri was incapable of moving to save himself and was burned to death.

Seeing the flames, neighbours rushed to the scene and among their number was a little old lady, who stood listening to Harri's dying screams. A few people in the crowd thought she looked like the old lady of the cottage.

Only a half-hearted attempt was made to deal with the fire, as the brother had been so hated and feared. While the inferno lasted the little old lady stood outside the farmhouse gate watching until the place was reduced to a smouldering heap. After giving what an onlooker described as a satisfied smile, she vanished, and a few people realised they had seen a ghost.

Through the years the ghosts of the two brothers are said to have walked occasionally on a dark night in winter around their former home and down to where the little old lady's cottage used to stand.

Call it coincidence or something supernatural: but the house that stands on the old farmhouse site has had its roof struck by lightning three times, but no-one has been injured.

The last time the lightning struck was in 1957.

THE SAD GHOSTS OF LUDLOW CASTLE

Among the ghosts haunting Ludlow Castle, which stands in Shropshire near the border of Wales, are those of a young, an old woman, and a young man.

The sixteen year old girl was the only daughter of the Lord of the Castle in the fourteenth century, and was idolised by her parents. Her love story, which caused her after her death to become an unquiet spirit, is almost like Shakespeare's Romeo and Juliet. Perhaps the Bard had heard the story of Sybille and taken it for a theme. She was madly in love with John, son of a family hated by her parents, and his parents in turn hated the girl's family. This situation meant the two lovers had to be extremely careful their meeting were not found out by either of their families, because it would without doubt lead to bloodshed.

Sybille had an old nurse who loved her dearly and it was with the old woman's connivance and some of the castle servants the lovers were able to meet frequently at the castle. While the two met and made love the servants kept vigilance, and both knew their secret was safe. The danger of perhaps being found out only added to the thrill of their meeting.

John, who was eighteen years old, seemed sometimes to Sybille to be rather reckless, laughing at her warnings of what would happen if her parents found out about him. She was terrified that the guardians of her father's castle would kill him. At the very least be would be badly wounded. When she voiced her fear to John his answer was always, "Do you think I would let them catch me, my dear little love", and then he would take her in his arms, whispering endearments. His answer would satisfy her for a while, but always deep inside her was the feeling one day tragedy would occur. Never in her wildest imagination was it the dreadful event that happened.

One evening after John came to her and as they lay in each other's arms he said, "There is really not much excitement in our meetings, is there, beloved?"

Puzzled, she asked him, "What do you mean?"

He went on to say, "Supposing it was more difficult for me to meet you, instead of having to sneak in and out of the kitchens and dungeons."

The girl laughed, "What are you talking about, my love? It is exciting enough for me to see you."

He then outlined a plan for her which she thought both silly and dangerous. She was to throw a very heavy rope from her bed chamber window and he would climb up it into her room. This idea was flatly turned down by Sybille at first, but before long John persuaded her.

He told her that in a few days' time her parents would be entertaining several friends by giving a feast in their honour. "I know because mine are invited," he said.

Most of the servants and guards would be on the opposite side of the Castle upon that night and there would not be anyone to see him climb the wall up to Sybille's bedroom. She was not very happy about the idea but she loved him too much to object. When the girl told her Nurse of this the old woman was horrified. "He will be killed, and you, my little love, will be sent to a Convent," she wailed.

In spite of her own misgivings Sybille told the old woman not to fear and all would be well. The girl had begged to be excused from attending the feast as she felt a fever coming on, and this was confirmed by her Nurse.

On the night of the feast, Sybille, helped by a servant and her old Nurse, dragged a heavy rope to the window of her room and lowered it carefully down. Before long the excited girl saw her lover's head appear above the edge of the window and she helped him into the room. By this time she too was enjoying the adventure, just as John had said she would. Quickly the pair threw off their clothing and snuggled down in the bed, drawing the bearskin rug coverlet over them. Between kisses they laughed at the novel way in which John had come to do his courting.

After they had finished their lovemaking, Sybille threw off the heavy cover and lay gazing sleepily around. What was that shadow in the twilight, surely not that of a man? There came more and more shadows and she realised the room was full of men carrying swords on their way to attack her parents and their guests, and to loot and pillage the Castle. Realising how she had been betrayed, Sybille jumped off the bed to pick up a dagger

John had left on the floor near her, as he hurriedly undressed.

Before he was aware of what the nearly crazed girl was going to do, she plunged the weapon with all her strength into his body, again and again. Within minutes he was dead, but still she went on striking at his body.

Covered in her lover's blood she ran screaming down to the dungeons below her room. Her old Nurse, hearing the screams, ran to the scene as fast as her aged limbs would let her.

Meanwhile the girl had reached the dungeons, and realising the blood-stained dagger was still in her hand, stabbed herself several times with it. Leaving a trail of blood she went through the dungeons and up on to the ramparts. With a cry she threw herself into the moat below.

The Nurse followed the trail of blood and found it ended at the ramparts. Knowing what her beloved charge had done, she too threw herself down into the moat and drowned.

So the two became sad ghosts, haunting the part of the Castle which Sybille had once occupied, and at times they have been seen near the moat. They throw their arms around each other and one spectre seems to be comforting its companion. On a still calm night people have thought they have heard the sound of wailing and have just been able to distinguish the words, "Forgive me, oh forgive me."

It has also been recorded from time to time that the ghosts of Sybille and her lover John have been seen in the streets of Ludlow during the evenings, walking hand in hand towards the Castle, both dressed in the fashion of the fourteenth century.

THE GHOST OF OWAIN GLYNDŴR

One of the most famous and revered chieftains of the Welsh nation was Owain Glyndŵr. He was born on the 28th May, 1354 and christened Owain ap Gruffydd Fychan and was of Royal Welsh descent on his father's side and of French royalty on his mother's. He preferred to be known as Owain Glyndŵr as most of his lands in Clwyd, North Wales, lay around the river Dyfrdwy.

The ancient chronicler Holinshed recorded that strange wonders took place at Owain's nativity. Horses in his father's stables stood kneedeep in blood. Shakespeare has Owain say:

> ". . .; at my nativity
> The front of heaven was full of fiery shapes,
> Of burning cressets; and at my birth
> The frame and huge foundation of the earth
> Shak'd like a coward."

> "To tell you once again that at my birth
> The front of heaven was full of fiery shapes,
> The goats ran from the mountains, and the herds
> Were strangely clamorous to the frighted fields.
> These signs have mark'd me extraordinary;
> And all the courses of my life do show
> I am not in the role of common men."

Owain Glyndŵr studied law in London and became a barrister. He returned to his favourite part of Wales, his country estate Sycharth. Before long, he entered into a feud with Earl Grey of Chester over land at Ruthin, which rightly belonged to Owain who fought over it and won.

Grey deliberately omitted to deliver a message from King Henry IV to Owain, with the result that Owain was declared a base traitor and the land in dispute given to Lord Grey. Owain immediately forsook the law to become a fighter for the freedom of Wales. He imprisoned Grey in Dolbadarn Castle, Llanberis, obtaining a huge ransom for his release from captivity. Thousands of young men joined Glyndŵr in battles all over

Wales. Students left Oxford and Cambridge to fight for Wales but in 1410 Glyndŵr's armies were defeated and thousands of warriors were killed, including French knights and soldiers who had come to assist the Welsh. After the last mammoth battle, Owain Glyndŵr vanished without trace. Historians said he died at Hereford in 1416 but this has never been verified.

Through the many years it has been rumoured that he has been seen in various places in Wales. His ghost was first recorded to have appeared close to Vale Crucis Abbey in Llangollen. The Abbot of Vale Crucis Abbey was taking a stroll in summer soon after dawn when he saw a figure dressed in warrior's clothing approaching him. Something told the Abbot he was seeing Glyndŵr's spirit. They talked for a while about banal subjects, then the Abbot said, "My Lord Glyndŵr why and where did you go when you disappeared? It is something your countrymen long to know, and above all whether you will return to drive the English oppressors from Wales?" With a wry smile Glyndŵr replied, "I shall keep the answers to myself." He went on to say, "But I can tell you that England will be ruled by kings of Welsh dynasty." He was of course, referring to the Tudors.

The Abbot wanted to question him further but the mist came down, and with a wave of his hand Owain Glyndŵr vanished. Shortly afterwards it cleared but the Abbot saw no sign of either ghostly or human figures around. Had he really seen the ghost of Glyndŵr, or had he only imagined seeing the ghost of the Welsh hero? He returned to his cell to pray for an answer. It must have been a favourable one because the Abbot spread the account of his meeting with the ghost far and wide.

The most recent sighting of the spectre of Glyndŵr was said to have been at Llandwrog, near Caernarfon by a friend of mine, a well known journalist. It was almost dusk and he was walking close to Belan, an old Roman fort, when he saw a tall figure which seemed to be wearing a long cloak, floating from its shoulders. Around its head there appeared to be a golden torque, such as ancient Welsh princes wore. The gleam of jewels was reflected by the dying rays of the sun.

It approached quite near to my friend and said, "Greetings my friend, how lovely is this part of my Wales. Hereford was lovely too but it was not surrounded by magnificent hills like these." My friend was about to start a conversation with the apparition when it vanished. He was convinced for the rest of his life he really had seen the ghost of Glyndŵr.

Owain Glyndŵr's memory is still revered by hundreds of young men and women of Wales. There was an accusation made against Owain: that he murdered his blood cousin Hywel Sele, Lord of Nannau. This his admirers strongly deny. They deny too that Glyndŵr was a magician although he studied the occult out of interest.

I do not think many of my Welsh readers will disagree with me when I say, nothing I have researched about Owain Glyndŵr points to the fact that he was a cold blooded murderer. As to the supposition he was a practising magician: "His magic lay in his fervent love for Wales which drove oppressed Welshmen to his side and his personal charisma which overflowed."

ANNAS AND THE ANGEL

Long ago in North Wales, there was, which is unbelievable today when you see the quiet rural surroundings when visiting Snowdonia, a large town in the vale of Gwynant, which went by the name of "The Vale".

Its inhabitants were wicked and ungodly. They did not believe in God and indeed they did not know anything about Him as Monasteries at this period in history were very few and far between in Wales. Monks used to visit occasionally, walking many, many miles to reach Nant Gwynant to try to tell the people who lived there about God. Sometimes the people of the town would listen to the monks, but at other times they would bar the gates of the town against them and throw large stones at the monks, telling them roughly to go away. The few townsfolk who had become Christians were frightened of letting others know, in case they would be attacked and even killed. The monks were brave men and dared the wrath of the ungodly people and entered the town in secret now and again. It had become really dangerous because the mood of the people had become ugly and they would not hesitate to kill the monks, perhaps slowly and painfully.

In the town was a pretty young girl called Annas (Agnes) who had become a Christian and she was very sad when the monks were jeered at and driven away with stones.

One particular day a young monk ventured into the town and began to preach.

Annas went up to him and said, "Holy man, please go away or they will surely kill you."

"Peace, my dear. Be not afraid for me. If they kill me my soul will go straight to God. If I die others will follow me. God will before long reveal his method of dealing with these wicked people. Leave me, or they might hurt you."

As he said this a gang of youths came along, laughing and jeering.

"Well, Holy man, give up your preaching and join us in drinking and doing whatever we please. We are not afraid of this man you call God."

The young monk started to preach and in a few minutes the

91

first heavy stone was hurled at him, striking him on the forehead. Then followed a hail of stones, which stopped when Annas rushed into the middle of the group, begging them to stop. Pausing just to push her roughly aside, as she was too pretty in their minds to kill, one youth was ordered to hold her. In sorrow and in terror the girl watched them kill the young monk by stoning and beating him to death with stout sticks.

When she was released Annas fled to her home, calling on God to witness the cruel murder of the young monk. That night she was weeping in her bed, unable to sleep thinking of the cruel way the monk had been murdered, when she heard a soft voice calling, "Annas, Annas". A bright light flooded her little room and there was an Angel in shining white garments. "Annas, Annas, you good and holy girl. God has sent me to carry you to safety." He said she was to go with him, as the doom of the town of Nant Gwynant was at hand.

Annas did not protest at leaving her home. Her parents had been killed some years before defending her from rape and she lived alone, so there was no member of her family to go with her. Gently the Angel stooped down, lifted the girl in his arms, and flew with her to Penygwryd, near the top of Llanberis Pass. There he placed her on a rock and said, "Fear not, kind girl, at what you will see tonight. It had to be done. Nant Gwynant refused salvation."

The Angel vanished and the girl looked towards her old home, and there a terrible sight met her eyes. Huge flames leapt into the air and the screams of the dying who were being consumed by the fires rang all around. All night long she prayed, and at dawn all she could see of the town was a great pile of ashes.

Praising and thanking God for her deliverance, Annas stayed near the rock for years, living alone. Eventually the rock, which is still there today, was called Gwastad Annas.

PHANTOMS OF LLANTWIT MAJOR AREA

Utterly devastated at murdering Prince Llywelyn, the last prince of pure Welsh lineage (known to his countrymen as *Llywelyn ein Llyw Olaf* (the last Helm), a Norman knight, Adam de Francton, left the English Army to retire to Llantwit Major. His properties were called Great and Little Frampton as he had changed his name to Frampton in remorse at his evil deed.

He spent hour upon hour riding his great black stallion around his estates shouting, "I have dishonoured my knighthood in killing an unarmed man."

One night, he rode more recklessly than usual; he was thrown by his horse and breaking his own neck, died instantly. The accident happened opposite the main gate of Great Frampton. Records relate that for hundred of years afterwards, the knight's ghost with its neck lolling, rides the snorting black battle destrier outside the main gate of Great Frampton. At times only the sound of thundering horse's hooves, with an occasional sound of something heavy falling to the ground are heard, but no phantom appears.

Until recent years, local residents did not care to linger near where the accident happened in case they heard or saw, what was known as the Frampton horse.

Near the gate there was supposed to be another phenomenon, in the form of a huge red-eyed yellow mastiff which rattled the chains securing it to a wall. In the next field to the dog there was supposed to be a huge man dressed in black who carried a pitchfork with which it tossed burning hay all around.

It was no use to the brave who wanted to see the man or the mastiff turning up at specific times: the two spectres only manifested themselves to people who happened to be passing and had not even heard of them.

The old folk of the area uttered a warning to anyone who walked through the meadow next to where the ghost threw burning hay around. Should they do so, they might not be able to find their way out for five or six hours and the search for an exit could drive them permanently mad.

Sitting on a stile about a mile from Frampton village, a huge man dressed in black (but not the man mentioned in this tale as haunting the field by Great Frampton gates) was to be seen contemplating the West, at intervals turning his head completely in a circle as if unable to control its movement. Until the murder of Llywelyn, the whole area had always been quiet, except for the occasional battle between the Welsh and English, and free from supernatural tales. To the superstitious it was as if the Prince's murder had disturbed the sleep of many of the dead. They became spectres to terrify the living. The ghosts not only manifested singly but in groups.

Nearby Llanfaes village has a typical example of group haunting. Just outside the village was a road known locally as 'Gallows' Walk' which had a gibbet at the end of it, and the ghosts of the unhappy prisoners were seen to walk slowly and reluctantly up that grim road. Ghostly dogs of all shapes and sizes (not the Devil Dogs which are hounds) but dogs who appeared to be looking for their doomed masters and these dogs whined pathetically. Near the old gallows heavy thuds could be heard sometimes.

About a quarter of a mile up the Gallows' Road there was a deserted chapel called Bethesda and opposite it a haunted house named Froglands. Both buildings were said to be haunted. Locals said it was a frightening experience to walk along the road leading to the chapel at night; the chapel was full of a blue light. After the murder, hundreds of ghostly worshippers tried to make their way into the building. Anyone caught in this ghostly throng would be kicked, thumped and jostled if they dared to impede the phantom's progress. No one was daring enough; they crushed themselves into the hedgerows or jumped into fields. To the south of the haunted road more terrible scenes could be witnessed by the brave, but only once a year did the phenomenon appear.

This was on St Michael's Eve, September the twenty-ninth. Where grassland turns into craggy peaks is a *Cistfaen* (an ancient warriors' grave) near the remains of a Roman camp. A blue light appears just after mid-night and shines on the Roman camp site. It shines about the Cistfaen, more brightly than on the rest of the site. While the light shines, anyone brave enough to demand entry to the Cistfaen will witness an awesome never to be forgotten sight. The spectators will see a phantom battle between a Roman centurion and a Welsh chieftain. To gain entry the following must be said, "Pray let me come in to see who will win."

A local farmer's young son Llywelyn, consumed with curiosity by the old tale, climbed the crag. He sat down to rest where he could see the Cistfaen but all he saw was the moonlight streaming down. He fell asleep and awoke to the noise of battle.

The blue light was above the Cistfaen and the boy made haste to climb up to it. He looked into the warriors' grave and repeated the rhyme. At once, the air was filled with shrill cries. Hundreds of fearful spectres surrounded the boy, all pushing and jostling making their way into the grave. Their skeletal frames were horrible with the decay of centuries. Boney fingers clutched at him. What were once their faces were fixed in dreadful frozen grimaces.

From the centre of the Cistfaen came a blood-chilling cry answered by the spectres. From the centre of the blue light on the Cistfaen stepped a phantom Celtic warrior. Towards it came the spectre of a Roman centurion and both commenced to fight each other amidst cries of encouragement from the skeletons. It was at that point the boy saw the Celt fall and the Roman soldier draw a short sword from the Celt's body and hold it up. He waved it dripping with blood above his head. The ghostly spectators screamed in tribute to the victor. Out went the blue light; the moonlight took over again; the figures vanished and all was deadly quiet.

Llywelyn could barely scramble down the crags but he managed to reach his farmhouse home at dawn, shivering and terrified, almost unable to stand with cold. He could only burble about skeletons battling, then he collapsed. He was seriously ill for weeks. His friends and relatives said he had almost caused his own death by lying all night on the ridge. The doctor said he was suffering from severe shock and what is now called hypothermia. When he recovered, it was nearly twenty years before he could tell anyone the whole story of his uncanny experience in the Cistfaen.

THE MYSTERIOUS HOLLOW

It is not perhaps known to many visitors travelling along a section of the North Wales coastal road between Connah's Quay and Flint, Clwyd, that it was the subject of a poem written by Victorian poet Charles Kingsley. He used to rent a small cottage near Connah's Quay Harbour with a magnificent view across the river Dee.

It was opposite his front window overlooking the sands that the body of a beautiful dairymaid called Mary was washed ashore. She was herding the cattle home to a farm on the same side as Kingsley's cottage when she was drowned. In her memory he wrote his famous poem: "Mary call the cattle home across the sands o'Dee."

Where the body was found has been known locally for centuries as 'Edmund's Hollow'. The local Justice of the Peace had brought in a verdict of accidental death.

As far as the Hollow's history goes it did not matter what the season was or the weather, there was always a pocket of mist in the Hollow. Where the sands were it is now a busy dual carriageway and the hollow has almost been levelled out. One could enter into the mist which covered the whole road from both sides of the dip. The recent roadworks have reduced the indent and the occurrence of the mist.

Walking, riding a horse, cycle or driving a motor vehicle, as soon as the Hollow was entered a thick mist would come down suddenly but it cleared at the opposite side within a few minutes. Judging from the stories related to me, there seemed to be some uncanny force in the Hollow however no one has been badly injured or killed in any of the incidents reported.

Five years ago a friend of mine, an experienced driver, was driving along the main coast road on a fine sunny afternoon, travelling towards Flint on the correct side of the road. As she drove down into the hollow the sun was shining. Suddenly a thick black mist engulfed her. Something wrenched at her steering wheel and seemed to be forcing her to the wrong side of the road. The sun was still shining when she emerged from the mist and found that she was on the opposite side of the road with an on-coming car on a collision course with her. By some miracle, the cars missed each other. She told me of how scared she had been by the incident. "You would think that place was haunted," she remarked.

Another intriguing story was told to me by a Deeside business man whose father was involved in a strange incident in the Hollow. His father was cycling from Flint (where he ran one of the family businesses) to Connah's Quay. When he entered the Hollow the sun was shining brightly but as he cycled down into the hollow a black mist blanked out everything. Just before the mist appeared he was able to see a tall wraithlike figure cross in front of him. It appeared to pass to the rear of the cycle. His father swerved wildly and heard the sound of dreadful laughter.

The figure appeared again, just as his father reached the end of the Hollow. It gave another horrible laugh and deliberately crossed in front of the front wheel of the cycle. This time his father lost control of the machine and was catapulted straight across the road into a high hawthorne hedge. He sustained scratches and bruises and arrived home in a very shaken condition. He was forced to admit there must have been some supernatural force at work in Edmund's Hollow.

Through the years when the subject of Edmund's Hollow came up, people used to tell me that their parents and grandparents had said there was something supernatural about it.

Some told me when they cycled along the road, sometimes they felt as if the handles of their cycles were being pulled to one side. One girl told me she had been thrown on to the grass hedge for no reason at all and ended up cut and bruised. Another said she had seen a tall figure in the mist cross in front of her, then vanish. Pedestrians have said that in the Hollow, they have felt the urge to walk into the centre of the main road.

One day this year I was searching old documents at the Clwyd Records when I read about how smugglers in Georgian times had become such a menace on the Queensferry to Flint road that extra excise officers had to be recruited during the latter part of the year seventeen hundred. Among the names was that of an exciseman who had been appointed Chief Officer for the Connah's Quay-Flint district. His name was down as just 'Edmund' with no surname. So it would seem more than likely that this person could be the Edmund that the Haunted Hollow was named after.

AN ANNUAL AFFAIR

It was a day in the late spring of 1976, and a middle-aged Caernarfon woman set off accompanied by her dog on her favourite walk. This was across the Aber Bridge, opposite the Eagle Tower of Caernarfon Castle, where there is a right turn to a road running parallel with the shores of the Menai Straits.

After walking along it for two miles, she had almost reached the tiny church of Llanfaglan, set in the fields, with its ancient churchyard filled at this time of the year with primroses, when she paused to look back at the Isle of Anglesey. It seemed as if one could walk across the sand to Llanddwyn Island, shrine of Saint Dwynan, patron saint of lovers. Being a local woman, she knew this was not a journey to be tried, because there were dangerous, shifting sands.

It was such a clear day that the Irish Sea was visible to her left. All around there was silence, only broken now and again by the plaintive mew of a seagull, or the chirping of the oystercatchers and sandpipers.

She turned towards the church, thinking how pretty it was, when something caught her attention. It was the sound of many voices, and an occasional burst of laughter. Surely she could hear the tramp of marching feet, but whose, there was no-one in sight?

The noise was coming closer and closer, and she realised the marching feet were out of step, but there was still no sign of anyone. Her dog whined and cringed in fear, and it was then she saw them — a great crowd of men of all ages. Some wore elaborate Georgian dress, their wigs topped by flat tricorne hats, and carrying intricately decorated headed canes and pomanders. There were some wearing ragged clothing, golden hoops dangled from their ears, and gay coloured handkerchiefs were tied around their heads and they carried bundles on their shoulders. She noticed a minority seemed to be dressed like Victorian gentlemen. All, no matter whether poorly or grandly dressed, laughed and talked with each other.

Completely fascinated, the woman forgot her fear; she was too interested in finding out where they were all going.

On they marched (and she moved hastily out of their way), on and on towards the little church. In orderly fashion they trooped through the small lychgate of the churchyard. She was near enough to see over the low stone wall, and what she saw more than renewed her first feelings of fear. Each man chose a grave, then jumped on to it, and arms raised, sank into the earth. She realised afterwards some graves must have had flat stones on them.

Puzzled and somewhat distressed by what she had seen, the woman hurried home. Maybe it had been a daydream, but it had seemed so very real.

Much later, she told a group of friends about her unnerving experience. Among the listeners was an old man, born and bred in Caernarfon and then in his eighties. He knew something about the mystery.

"You know the Bar with its dangerous cross currents is just over there, and when the bodies from the wrecks in the Irish Sea were washed up on the beach near the church, it was impossible to know where all the drowned had come from, so they were buried in that little churchyard. Among them were corpses of pirates, and their tombstones have the 'skull and crossbones' carved upon them. The Rector at that time did not object to the irreligious carvings, probably out of fear of revenge by the former shipmates of the victims."

He said that his grandfather had told him that the ghostly walk had taken place annually for centuries, usually but not always in the month of June. He was certain that some of the victims of the Royal Charter wreck must surely have been in the parade.

It would seem as if some of ghostly participants were not buried in Llanfaglan Churchyard, because there could not possibly be enough room for all the victims of drowning tragedies within the walls of such a tiny area.

To the author, this has always been a delightful little church. She has seen the pirates graves. In season the tiny churchyard was filled with snowdrops and primroses.

In her young days in Caernarfon an annual service was held there by whoever was vicar of Caernarfon at the time.

THE SPECTRE ON THE WALL

From June to September you may be lucky (or unlucky) enough to come across a ghostly figure walking along the sea wall in the well-known North Wales seaside town of Prestatyn. Never has this phenomenon been reported except in the holiday season. The figure seems to prefer walking the sea wall just before dark in June, and continues haunting until mid September.

There is no record of this section of the coast road having once been the site of a Convent. It is not certain the figure is the spectre of a nun, and the record of the sitings did not begin until about twenty years ago. It has been christened by the local residents; 'The White Lady'.

In the higher part of Prestatyn, one or two burial grounds dating from Roman and Norman times have been discovered, some within the last decade, but it hardly seems feasible that even a ghost would make such a long trek to haunt the sea wall.

1975 was the time of the modern maxi dress, so to see a woman in a long white dress certainly did not draw a Rhyl's man's thoughts to ghosts, but he is convinced that what he saw was a ghost.

He was very fond of taking his dog for an evening stroll along Prestatyn sea front. That particular evening he pulled up his car at the usual stopping place and put the dog on a lead and set off to follow the sea wall. He had not been walking more than a few minutes, admiring the end of a glorious sunset, when he saw in front of him, coming towards him, the tall slim figure of a lady dressed in a long white dress. She had on her head what he took to be a long white scarf. He did think it was rather late for a lady to be taking a lone stroll. Then he became preoccupied with the dog, as it was, like many of its breed, of uncertain temperament and was behaving oddly, so he bent down to tighten its lead, in case it attacked the woman because of her dress. As he straightened up he felt a strong tug on the lead. The dog had crouched low and was shivering and shaking. He patted it and told it not to be silly, but it howled and jumped into his arms.

The figure, which had the whole time been walking at a steady pace, suddenly began walking much faster. With a yowl of terror the dog sprang from his arms, snapping the lead, and turned back to make a dash for the car. By then the man did not feel too happy and was expecting something to happen.

On and on towards him came what he now knew to be a ghost.

It was dressed in a nun's habit. He ventured to look and was horrified to find it did not have a face, only an empty space where the face should have been. He was powerless to move at all. All around the air had become icy and he felt incapable of coherent thinking.

The apparition continued to approach, and either she walked straight through him or vanished into the air just before touching him. He cannot even now remember what really happened to the figure and does not particularly want to. Even after her disappearance the air stayed icy for a short while.

Somehow he got to the car, where his dog was huddled under the front wheel.

The man was badly shaken and it was a while after he got home before he was able to tell his wife of his experience, as much as he could recall. Their conversation opened with his wife saying, "Joe, you look as if you had seen a ghost."

His reply was, "You are so right, dear."

She believed his story, and in her opinion he seemed the last person to think he had seen a phantom. In any case, she had heard there was a ghostly nun at Prestatyn.

"He does believe in ghosts now," she says, and tells people about what happened when he took their dog for its evening stroll.

THE HAUNTINGS AT BERAIN

At Llannefydd, Clwyd, stands a very old Manor called Berain, where Catrin Tudor, a kinswoman of Queen Elizabeth I, lived. In her teenage days she had lived happily for a time at the Queen's Court. She died when she was about fifty years old in 1591 and had so many descendants of noble birth that she earned the nickname of *Mam Cymru* (The Mother of Wales). There are horrific legendary stories about the way in which she murdered her seven husbands. The fact that she was married seven times has never been corroborated; but there are records of four marriages.

One story tells of how she was proposed to when she was returning from the funeral of her first husband, a proposal which she refused, but said if she was to marry for the third time, it would be to him. She had already agreed to wed Sir Richard Clough on the outward journey to the funeral reported one ancient chronicle.

The method she was supposed to have used to murder all seven husbands was said to be the pouring of molten lead into their ears while they were in a drugged sleep. She arranged to have them buried at the dead of night in the orchard at Berain. It was also rumoured that she used this horrible method to kill a few lovers when she got tired of them, and they too were buried in the orchard.

To have buried all her husbands in the orchard is ridiculous, as it is a very small orchard. There is positively no record of any of these bodies ever being exhumed.

Up to the 18th century there were tales of the orchard being haunted ever since Catrin died. There have been accounts of ghostly figures being seen in the hours of night flitting in between the trees in the orchard. All around Berain there was alleged to have been heard the sound of wailing. Several times there have been reports of a headless horse galloping around in the grounds of Berain. What it had to do with the ghosts relating to Catrin is without credibility.

Inside the Manor, two walls of one room were covered with bloodstains and as soon as they were laboriously removed, within twenty-four hours they reappeared. The theory was that

Catrin, in attempting to murder one of her husbands, had met with fierce resistance, probably because he had not been sufficiently drugged. This meant she had possibly used a dagger to kill him. However she was never brought to trial for murder.

Legend also says that the spectre of a woman dressed in the fashion of Elizabethan times walked in the past through the rooms of Berain, and sometimes could be seen outside the front of the Manor. The figure walked about with head bowed and clasping and unclasping its hands, uttering a pitiful moan. It might be that Catrin's spirit could not rest in its grave because of the dreadful and untrue tales that had been spread about her during and after her lifetime.

With a friend I visited Berain a few years ago. It was then owned by a hospitable farming couple, who showed us around. It is a charming example of the Elizabethan period, with wonderful wood carvings of the Tudor Rose on the panels of a magnificent staircase. I did not observe any blood stains.

They said Catrin's ghost had never appeared to them and they felt at ease always. When we entered the original part of the farmhouse and saw Catrin's private apartment, there was a peaceful, serene atmosphere prevailing in it. One could imagine her sitting sewing in her room. Then, when we came to the section where the original staircase in perfect condition stood, the atmosphere seemed to change and become almost sinister. It became cold, although it was mid June.

It seems almost impossible to believe that Catrin of Berain was the instigator of the foul murders attributed to her. Could she have been a target for jealous rumours? She was a very attractive and highly-connected woman with a somewhat tragic history. Her son was executed for his part in the Babbington plot to murder her kinswoman Queen Elizabeth I. That was a terrible shock to Catrin which she never fully recovered from.

THE STILE

A recently constructed by-pass swallowed up in its wake part of a haunted path behind the Shire Hall buildings in Mold. It led to the tiny hamlet of Sychdyn and came out near the outskirts of Northop village.

There used to be an old stile separating the path from the fields but during the last few years it has been removed. It was near this stile that a ghost was said to stand; sometimes it would walk up and down the path.

The alleged appearance of the ghost dates back to a tragic happening during the first part of the Victorian era. Many local people reported sighting the spectre frequently up to the First World War. After this period only a very few reported seeing anything supernatural in that area for several years. Then as if something had disturbed the spirit, it restarted haunting, making an appearance every three or four years. The last sighting was by a man from Mold in 1979 but he could not describe the apparition. He said it was very faint in outline.

The ghost is supposed to be that of a young dairy maid who used to work at a Sychdyn farm. It wears a grey coloured dress of the Victorian period which is partially covered by a large white apron. On its head is a mob cap, such as female farm servants in those days used to wear. Around its shoulders is a short grey shawl which it has been seen to hug around itself. Other times it has been seen to clutch its throat convulsively.

Those who have been close enough to see the face were struck by the terrified look on it. Some of the persons alleged to have seen this ghost said it seemed to make a low moaning sound, very scaring to hear.

The recorded story behind this haunting is one of the love of a young girl for the son of a farmer who lived close to where she worked.

This young man was expected by his family to marry the daughter of a wealthy landowner in the district. It was obvious that he did not love the little dairy maid as he never mentioned anything to her about the other girl. One of the servants who worked with her said her lover was betrothed to another girl. She just laughed and thought it was jealousy on the part of the servant to tell her this, and never asked him if he was faithful.

The lovers used to meet most evenings at the stile and then make their way to a small wood nearby, where they found a secluded spot to make love on warm spring and summer nights. In the winter, they used to meet each other in an old barn near the young man's home.

One evening she met her lover at the stile as usual and she seemed very quiet, having little to say. After teasing her for her silence he managed to make her tell him why. She told him she was pregnant and asked him when they would marry. He became terribly angry and stormed at the girl telling her he had been pledged to another for several months. While she tearfully reproached him, his anger grew and he strangled her. Carrying her body into a nearby copse, he dug a shallow grave, covering it with leafmould.

The next day the lightly covered grave was discovered by a game-keeper's dog out with his master. By the end of that day the young man was in goal. He stood trial for murder, was found guilty of the crime and hanged at Chester.

In many stories of murder the victim becomes a ghost, seeking vengeance by exposure of the criminal. In this case as the murderer was caught and hanged it does not supply the motive for this sad little ghost to haunt in an effort to obtain justice.

As for the murderer there have been vague reports near this particular place that his ghost haunts the scene of the crime. The apparition is that of a young man dressed in the fashion of the same period as the little dairy maid. The murderer has a motive for haunting — remorse for his evil deed.

This ghost wanders along the path, but turns sharply within a few feet of the stile, then disappears. It has also been reported as being seen behind Theatr Clwyd and Llwyn Egryn, both part of the Shire Hall complex.

REFLECTIONS IN THE POOL

There is a stretch of road between Pentre Halkyn and Milwr which runs above the top coast road leading to the North Wales resorts. Up to the present day, people living in this area are very reluctant to use the section of this road called *Rhyd Fudr* (the dirty ditch) on dark wintry nights. This is the area where the Romans used to have lead mines and was the site of the court of one of the ancient princes of Wales.

The outline of centuries-old spectres have become fainter and fainter but other phenomena, icy atmosphere and so on, accompanying these sightings, never seem to vary.

This appears to be true about the part of the road called Rhyd Fudr. At a place which is called *Caeau Mine* (fields of the mine) there was once a farmhouse, long since destroyed. Right opposite where the gates to the farmhouse used to stand, the road begins to dip. There is always a small amount of water in this dip, summer or winter. Motorists have told of the strangely-shaped reflections to be seen where the car's headlights shine as the vehicle approaches the dip. Some of these travellers say they have seen white reflections, other say the water gives the impression of something very dark and grotesque in shape.

It may be that some of these people, knowing of the old ghost story associated with this spot, have let their imagination run riot. The old story tells how, one dark winter's night about 300 years ago, a monk was making a journey to Basingwerk Abbey, not far from Holywell. He had with him some gold, destined for the abbey. The next day the monk was found lying in the Dirty Ditch having been brutally murdered, and all the gold he carried was missing.

Many accounts of seeing the ghost of the murdered monk have been given, dating from a few months after the murder right up to a few years ago. He is described in early records as being tall with the cowl of his robe folded down at the back of his shoulders. His face looked pale and he wrung both his hands in agitation and seemed to be looking for something on the ground.

The last person to have seen this apparition said he could only see the faint shape of the monk, but he was so frightened he turned and ran towards his home without attempting to take a closer look.

GHOSTS OF RUTHIN

It was near the Kissing Gate at Ruthin a miner some twelve years ago said he saw a troop of phantom miners about four foot in height coming towards him along a narrow footpath. They were led by two monks, both over seven feet tall, and dressed in black. As they came nearer he realised with horror they were all faceless. He was terrified and instinctively tried to turn and run back the way he had come, but was petrified on the spot. The ghostly procession advanced on and on towards him and he made a supreme effort and jumped into the nearest hedge, where he fainted in fright. He was alone when he came to and he ran home, arriving dishevelled and covered with cuts and bruises. His relatives wrote to the author telling of the uncanny happening.

An archaeological dig a few years ago, near where this ghostly procession was seen, unearthed several small skeletons and two very tall ones. No doubt there had been a burial ground adjacent to the Castle.

The Ruthin Castle Hotel is reputed to have a ghost, not frequently seen by anyone. It might add extra entertainment to the Castle Hotel mediaeval banquets if it appeared more often. It is a knight in chain armour who seems to be searching for something. Could it be a missing gauntlet, as he appears to be wearing only one protective metal gauntlet? The accounts describing the apparition point this out, so it must be the spectre of a knight who lived after about 1150, as the Normans added gauntlets to their armour just after the middle of the twelfth century.

The spectre enters one of the rooms of the Hotel through the wall and makes it exit the same way. It is perfectly silent on each occasion and has a rather cross expression.

About eight years ago a Ruthin lady wrote to the author, telling of the uncanny experience of her aged mother, who lived opposite Ruthin Castle. She wrote, "My mother is certain she saw a ghost last year. She was seated at a table opposite her window in front of the Castle." Suddenly she saw a Georgian Dandy walking slowly up her garden path. He wore a tricorne hat and swept it off his head as he bowed to her. "Not a bit afraid, my mother got up from the table to get a better look, but the apparition vanished before she could open the door in the hope of a chat," as she put it.

No other member of her family had ever seen a phantom.

THE TRAGIC LOVERS OF FLINT

Flint has two traditional ghosts — and a few modern ones.

The location where the two traditional ghosts are said to haunt still is around the former site of Flint Manor Farm, which was opposite the recently-closed Crosville Bus Depot.

Some years ago there was a report of a sighting of two ghostly figures moving around the rear of the parked buses. Two employees told how, late one summer night, just as they were getting their cars out to go home after late duty, they thought they saw someone standing behind a bus. They made out the figure to be that of a girl wearing a long dress, with her head covered by a shawl. Within a few seconds she was joined by another figure, but the two men could barely see it. They left their cars with the intention of warning any unauthorised person against tampering with any of the vehicles. To their amazement, before they had reached half way towards the figures, they seemed to spiral off the ground and disappear.

During the eighteenth and last century there were reports of two apparitions walking along the road near the entrance to the farm. The spectres are thought to be those of a young couple who lived at the end of the eighteenth century and were in love but whose love story ended tragically. There is no record of either of their names.

She was the sixteen-year old daughter of the Squire who lived at Flint Manor, which has long gone out of existence. He was a young labourer employed by the tenant farmer of Flint Manor Farm.

For some months they had been meeting secretly, and then the Squire got to hear of the romance. He was furious and warned the farmer that he would be deprived of his tenancy if he did not send the young man away. The farmer was very reluctant to do this as the young man was an excellent worker. On the other hand, he was too much afraid of the Squire not to carry out his order. The angry father kept his daughter locked up in the Manor until her lover had been sent away.

It was about a week after the farmer had been told to get rid of the young man when the Squire's daughter managed to escape and meet her lover. The two lovers had no means of going away together, and time was running out, as the girl's father would not remain patient much longer. The girl tearfully told her lover that her maid had that evening heard of the Squire's decision to force the farmer to throw the young man out the next day. The young man refused to subject the girl to the hardships of the road by running away with her, in spite of her frantic pleas.

The next morning he left and, when the girl heard of this, she took action. Her father that day had told her she was free to go out again, but she did not speak to him.

The following morning, when her maid went to call her, she found the girl lying lifeless on the bed. She had plunged a dagger into her heart, striking so hard and deliberately that only one thrust had been necessary.

The young man had left the farm but not the district, as he wanted to stay near and get a glimpse of his love. Daringly, he called at the farm, to visit his former employer. The farmer, his family and the servants were reluctant to tell him of the tragic death of the girl, but finally one of them plucked up the courage to do so. With a cry he rushed out of the house and the farmer thought he had run off. It was not until the next day his body was found hanging in one of the barns.

For a year or two he haunted the farmyard and the building where his body had been found. This frightened the people living at the farm so much that they called in a local clergyman to exorcise the unquiet spirit. This seemed to be successful as far as the farm was concerned but, before long, the ghost materialised again. This time it haunted the manor grounds and the immediate vicinity. Before long this ghost was joined by another, that of the squire's daughter.

WHO CHANGED THE WORDS?

Some persons possessed of extra-sensory powers have come across spirit writing from time to time. This is a true account of what one Caernarfon woman saw and of what happened in 1937. It is something she will never forget.

She lived in a big house where a friend of her grandfather had made his home with the family for many years. A bachelor, he was a well-known person in political circles, a former Member of Parliament, and he treated her as his daughter. He was the first person to whom the midwife handed the baby. The child was utterly spoilt — nothing was too good for her. He paid for her education at a well-known Convent in South Wales. She was constantly at his side at political meetings when she had left school. He imparted his wisdom to her, and introduced her to many famous political and titled figures of those days. No young man was good enough for her in his opinion.

When he was just on the right side of sixty, he became very ill. It became necessary to have a day and a night nurse, as he suffered from heart disease towards the end. A few weeks prior to his death, his only brother, David, died. His death was very sudden as the result of a heart attack. The police where his brother lived delivered a note to the sick man informing him of this.

A month later, on a Sunday evening, the young woman decided to turn out a drawer in the kitchen which was always crammed full of papers. Her adoptive father when she had seen him earlier, spoke to her and seemed better. The nurses had not changed shifts and all was quiet in the lounge on the second floor which had been adapted as a bedroom.

The young woman had cleared one drawer. She had started on the second drawer when a piece of paper caught her eye. She pulled it out and recognised it as the note from the Police. She said to her aunt, "I thought this note had been destroyed." She looked at it and began to read, "The Superintendent regrets Mr X died tonight." The words had changed from Mr X's brother, and the date read that night, not a month previously. The name stood out clearly as 'Robert' not 'David'. The young woman screamed "Oh God" and ran up the stairs to the bedroom.

She was just in time to put her arms around Mr X as he died from a heart attack. Heartbroken she cried, "He was the first to hold me when I came into this world and I was the last to hold him as he left it."

She never found the note again, nor the reason why the name had changed. Her aunt read the note and the original words were on it. She told the young woman this years afterwards, and that she had burnt it.

She said, "I believe you, that you saw the changed note, or how could you have gone to him." To her the writing had not changed.

It is not possible to give the true names in this story.

REGENCY LADY

From a very early age Stanley had been able to predict happenings occasionally, but had given this very little thought. As he approached his middle teens he began to think he must possess psychic powers. He never mentioned this in case his friends laughed at him.

He lived in the small North Wales town of Connah's Quay, where nothing happened after sunset to cause anyone to be afraid of walking around. Entertainment for Stanley and his contemporaries in those days of the 1950 to 60 era consisted of a weekly visit to the local cinema accompanied by the current girl friend, church socials, and the weekly Saturday night hop. There was plenty of competition among the local lads for the pleasure of escorting the girls home from the dances. Girls were very partial to Stanley's fair hair and good looks and he was well aware of this and constantly changing his girlfriends.

With the psychic feelings he had there were certain areas of the town he was not too fond of walking in late at night and in the early hours of the morning. There was one particular spot opposite the local Drill Hall on the hill where he lived where he had, on a few occasions, felt as if someone was standing watching him, but the someone or something never followed him, until one night.

He was returning from a late night dance after seeing a young lady to her door when once again passing the Drill Hall he not only felt a presence, but saw a great black blob of no definite shape and felt the dreadful fear of something evil. The thing began to follow him; he increased his pace, and so did the pursuer. Over to Stanley's account in his own words.

"I began to run and so did it, and I now knew that evil was around and all I could do was say a prayer. Faster and faster I ran up that hill and my home seemed to get further and further away and I knew that if the black blob caught up with me it would possess my soul. I strove in my tangled thoughts to remember whether my mother had said she would leave the front door unlocked, putting the key under a stone near the door step. Only a few minutes now and I would be safe inside my home and could dip my fingers into the bowl of Holy water hanging on the wall near the front door; mother was a devout Catholic. I reached the door and saw the shadow of the black thing on the door illuminated by the moon which had just broken through the clouds.

" 'Christ save me', I could feel the thing's hot breath on the back of my neck and I crashed against the door with just enough strength left to turn the knob on the door. It was unlocked and I stumbled into the hall and panting reached my fingers into the Holy water and I made the sign of the Cross before collapsing."

Stanley said it was fully two weeks before he went to a dance, and years before he walked alone at night up that hill. From then on Stanley believed himself psychic and was fully convinced by another not unpleasant supernatural encounter a year or so later.

He fell in love with a young girl from nearby Shotton who lived in Nelson Street. One afternoon he called at her house on his way home from the Steelworks. She met him, her face white. She told him she had heard queer sounds coming from a bedroom above the kitchen, and footsteps on the stairs. Stanley laughed and said he would go and find out whether there was anyone there. Up he went and just as he reached the top half of the stairs he felt very cold. This continued when he entered the bedroom and he knew a supernatural being was around. Stanley went downstairs and told the girl there was no-one there. He did not disclose his feelings about a ghostly presence.

"Must have been next door scuffling around," he said.

His girlfriend begged him to wait until her parents came home as she was still nervous, and he agreed. Before long her parents returned, just as Stanley was finishing his tea.

Later, while it was still fairly light he got ready to leave, and kissed his girlfriend. Her father, who also worked at John Summers, told Stanley he wanted a word about an Union matter. She left them talking at the front door and joined her mother in the kitchen. As they talked standing close to the front door opposite the stairs, Stanley felt again the same intense cold as previously. He turned and there, at the top of the stairs stood a young woman in a Regency dress; she had a pale, pretty face, but this prettiness was marred by an expression of terror.

As Stanley had broken off the conversation, his girlfriend's father turned towards the stairs, and he too saw the ghost.

"My God, Stan, don't tell the women if you saw what I have just seen."

"Yes, I am sure I saw a girl in an old-fashioned dress," said Stanley.

Later his future father-in-law told him that once a member of the family said he had seen the spectre but thought he had imagined it.

Stanley knew the manifestation was a harmless one but was filled with curiosity as to whom the ghost had been when it was alive. He enquired amongst a few of the older people living in Nelson Street what they remembered about the street. He was told that many years before Nelson Street came into being the land was just waste land and was the scene in Georgian times of a murder. A young local girl of good family made a tryst with her lover, who was a gipsy, and on the spot where Stanley's girlfriend's house was eventually built, he had strangled the girl. The ghost appeared several times after the two men had seen it and it was not long before the rest of the household got to know of the manifestation. The family were not too keen to share the house with a ghost, and soon after Stanley and his girlfriend married, her parents moved.

This particular house in Nelson Street is still said to be haunted.

THE SEVERED HAND

Stan Clarke was very fond of hiking, particularly in Wales, mostly following unbeaten tracks. His home was in Lancashire, but his heart seemed to be in Wales, and whenever he could find time he made his way to whichever part of Wales was within reach.

He had spent all day walking in the hills round Bala and had just passed through a tiny village which had one pub, a general shop, and two, if not three, Methodist Chapels. He enjoyed a couple of pints of real Welsh ale at the pub before he went on his way.

When he was a short distance from the pub he found a narrow lane facing him. He walked about a hundred yards up this lane and saw a small cottage. The path leading to the cottage was overgrown with weeds, giving the place a neglected appearance. There did not seem to be anyone around, although he thought he saw washing fluttering in the breeze on a line at the back of the cottage. There was not even the usual clucking of hens to be heard, or the bark of a dog.

He decided to go to the back door and knock. There was no answer, so he looked through the window.

The room inside was furnished in Victorian country style, although the year was 1972. There was a round table in the centre of the room, covered with a red check tablecloth. Above the old Welsh fireplace hung a huge smoked ham and a string of onions. He pressed his face to the window pane to get a closer look. He saw the table was set for one and there was an unfinished meal on this table. Then, to his surprise he saw a young oak tree growing up through the floor on one side of the kitchen. To add to his surprise, he saw that the tree had pushed up through the kitchen ceiling.

"No use hanging around this cottage," he thought to himself, although there was an unfinished meal on the table, which meant the owner was not far away.

What sort of people would let a tree grow through their kitchen floor, he wondered. Oh well, none of his business and he really had to find his way and find shelter for the night. He set off down the path again and looked to the left and saw a short

117

distance away the figure of a woman. He went towards her and to his horror saw that her left hand was severed so badly that only a few sinews held it together. The blood was pouring down her clothing.

"Oh my God, I am coming" he yelled. At this the woman turned and ran away.

His one thought was he must get help. The woman would die and she was too hysterical to let him near her. Stan raced off back to the little pub, crashed through the door until it swung wildly on its hinges.

"Quickly, quickly, she will die!" he shouted to the startled customers. "Get an ambulance, she will not let me help her. She is up the lane."

Instead of rushing to do as he asked, the people in the bar sat silently and the landlord said, "What is she like, lad?"

"What is she like, how do I know? Move, damn you!" Stan screamed.

To his shocked amazement the landlord said calmly, "Sit down, lad. Here, Billy, pour him a drink."

Billy poured out a whiskey and brought it from behind the bar to Stan.

"Down with it," said Billy.

Stan pushed the drink away. "Oh, God, why don't you go and help her?" he moaned.

"No use, lad, it is too late. She is dead."

"How do you know? It has only just happened, and none of you have gone to help," said Stan.

The answer came slowly from the landlord. "She died a long time ago, poor young thing. How long was it, Billy? Ten years ago, or is it eleven or twelve now?"

"I am mad or you are all mad," gasped Stan.

"None of us is mad and neither are you," said the landlord. "Calm down a little, drink up and Billy here will tell you about the woman you saw."

About five minutes later Stan was able to listen to what Billy had to say.

"The woman you saw was the ghost of Esther, who was once the wife of Ivor Thomas, who lived in that cottage you must have called at. Esther was an attractive girl of seventeen, the daughter of a poor farmer who lived in the district. She used to go to Ivor's cottage to clean for him, and he thought what a good wife she would make. He went to see her parents, and they were delighted at Esther's "good luck", as they put it. The girl did not want to marry this middle-aged man, and said so in no uncertain manner. Finally her parents' pleadings so wore her down, she consented. 'Silly girl to think of refusing such a man, nearly a Reverend he is,' said her mother. Big man in the Chapel too, and well off,' added her father. The couple were married and Ivor took his young bride home to the cottage.

"This was the start of a life of Hell for the girl. Ivor was mean and cruel. He kept Esther short of food and had her slaving on his smallholding while he went to the local markets and prayer meetings. When she knew a baby was on its way, the girl was heartbroken. She knew the baby would get as hard a life as she had. She decided to steal a few eggs every day, and these she hid amongst the bracken near her home. After Ivor had gone off for the day, she collected the eggs and sold them in the village, mostly to the landlord of this pub. She only managed to hoard a few shillings to buy clothes for the expected child. The baby duly arrived, a lovely little boy, but this did not change Ivor. He was just as mean and cruel as ever. 'One bloody more mouth to feed' he often shouted at the terrified girl.

"She became frantic, and one day took the baby to a friend's house in the village, telling her she would not be away long. Esther went to the cottage and got a large sharp knife. There, in the spot where you saw her ghost, she hacked at her wrist, severing it. No-one was about so she died from loss of blood.

"Ivor was not too unhappy, although he made a great show of being so. The baby was given to relatives to look after.

"On the Sunday three days after his wife's funeral, Ivor was sitting at the table in the kitchen of the cottage. He had placed on this table a cloth containing the day's offerings at the local chapel (where he was Senior Deacon and Treasurer), and some bread and cheese and pickle for his supper. But the next day he had gone to a relative's house to stay. He left everything on the table just as it was, half finished meal and chapel takings.

"He never visited the place again. Within a month or so, he had some of the furniture sent to the house where he was staying. Not long after it was installed, the furniture, which consisted of a fine old Welsh dresser and a corner cupboard, started to move

119

about the room of its own accord. During the night it could be heard, bumping about. The next day the furniture was sold. Ivor never told anyone what he had seen that Sunday night in his cottage while he sat at his supper. No-one dared ask him — he was a very violent man. In a way the villagers thought they knew. Esther had come back to haunt him, or otherwise why should such a mean man leave everything and go away. Perhaps it was Satan himself who had visited."

After a while, when he could think clearly again, Stan recalled the washing on the line had been rotten and the ham hanging from the beam looked dried up. He thanked the landlord, and Billy for telling him the sad tale, and ever after that believed in ghosts.

I myself some years ago saw this cottage and the young oak sapling was growing straight and tall through the cottage roof.

In 1978 Stan dared to revisit the little cottage. It was now partly in ruins and the oak sapling was a tree. This time Esther's ghost did not appear, and he learned when he called in again at the little pub that the previous year Ivor had died. Hearing this, Stan became quite fanciful and imagined that perhaps Esther had haunted her husband for some time but now that he was dead the need was finished.

The account of the suicide is definitely true but I had to wait until Ivor was dead to tell this grim tale.

WREXHAM GHOSTS

Charles Street, Wrexham is a narrow street leading from the centre of the town down to the Eagle's Meadows (now the site for superstores) and what used to be known as the beast market. In olden days people would at times crowd into Charles Street enroute to witness a public hanging. The gallows stood on what is now a large traffic island.

The area was always said to be haunted. One of the buildings there was a leather mill and a rich owner was reputed to have walled up one of his servants alive in a small room in the building. This inhuman man did not make known his reason for this extreme and ultimate punishment. He might have read about this horrifying practice being carried out in ages past by religious orders and thought it a good idea.

In Victorian times, the mill was converted into a bakery and various strange occurences were reported there, indicating poltergeist activities. Ovens would light up by themselves, at other times all the bread would burn. Sometimes yeast would be spoiled, also fresh loaves would be damaged. Through the years reports of haunting gradually diminished until about a year ago. It is about then rebuilding and renovation of the area around Charles street began. The excavation of foundations, knocking down walls and other activities seem to have disturbed the spirits and there has been an increase in accounts of alleged manifestations.

At the start of 1989, the body of a man was found in the rear garden of one of the premises. Apparently the cause of death was a heart attack. Some of the locals say there was a horrified expression on the face of the corpse and they began to wonder if he had come face to face with one of the wandering ghosts and died from shock.

The first and second floors of the one time mill, and then a bakery, are now two residential flats. One of the flats is occupied by two young women students. Independently, both have heard strange noises but did not compare notes until a very short time ago. The noises usually consisted of heavy footsteps walking along the corridor, tapping on doors and a heavy thud or two. None of this phenomena happened when the two girls were together.

For example, recently, one was in bed reading when there was a tapping on her door. She called on her friend to come in and when she did not do so she got up and opened the door. There was no one there, or on the landing. She went down the stairs into the living room and her friend was sitting at the table typing where, she said she had been for the past half hour.

The friends were helping the landlord decorate their flat. When the paper was stripped from the wall of the bedroom of which the door had been mysteriously tapped, they found an area of wall which had obviously been blocked off a long time ago.

On working out the dimensions of the room the girls calculated there was a small area over the corridor and the staircase which was puzzling as it did not seem to be necessary. Could there be a connection with the story of the sadistic employer and the unfortunate servant?

Despite these recent happenings the girls are not afraid of any threat of evil or even mischief from their resident spirit. They call him "Dick" and hope that once the rebuilding of the area has been completed the restless spirits will leave them in peace.

* * *

There are a few residents of Wrexham who believe they have recently seen the manifestation of one of Wales's most revered martyrs, Saint Richard Gwyn, who was born in Llanidloes, mid Wales, in the year 1557.

He was brought up in the Protestant faith and after leaving Oxford university he finished his university career at Cambridge in 1562 and returned to Wales. He began to teach in schools around Wrexham and was converted to the Catholic faith while instructing at a school in Overton-on-Dee near Wrexham. Because of his conversion he had to flee from one school after another to escape persecution from the Protestants.

He was captured in Wrexham in 1579 but escaped. In July 1580, he was caught for the last time and was kept in prison for four years. On the 9th October 1584 he was convicted of high treason. On the 17th October of the same year he was hanged drawn and quartered on the site of what is now a large traffic roundabout. A holy relic consisting of the hand of St Richard was found shortly after his martyrdom on the site where he met his

122

death. His head was displayed at Wrexham, on a Pike. It is said that Rome regards him as the first martyr in North Wales. In December 1989 the author was told by two informants, of the alleged manifestation of a spectre which might be that of the Martyr Saint Richard Gwyn but has been asked not to name them.

The spirit has a benevolent expression and raises its hands in blessing. The vision has appeared around midnight but the story has made her nervous of publishing it, in case the story attracts too much publicity.

Richard Gwyn was cannonised on the 25th October 1970 and pupils from St. Richard Gwyn High School, Flint were taken to the ceremony in Rome in the charge of the senior master Mr G McCormick. Every year (within one or two days of the date of the anniversary of the Martyrdom of St Richard Gwyn) the school holds a Rememberance Walk in honour of its Patron Saint.

Since completing this book, it is alleged the ghost of the Saint has been seen a few weeks ago that is at the end of March 1990. The hour has again been given as around midnight. It seems strange this phenomenon has never been reported until the end of 1989 and that the Press has not featured it.

HAUNTINGS AT EWLOE CASTLE

Historians do not know for certain, when the now three-parts ruined castle of Ewloe, which is in the Parish of Hawarden, was built.

It is easily reached from Connah's Quay by walking through a charming woodland path leading from Wepre Park. The entrance to the park is less than three minutes by car from the main coast road at Connah's Quay.

Records say that it was not built by the Welsh but the Normans in the 11th century as a Manor, the manorial rights including lands of Wepra or Wepre. In the middle of the 12th century it is recorded that the great Welsh Prince, Owain Gwynedd, built a castle on the ruins of this Manor. When he died his son Dafydd inherited the Castle, but it had not been in his possession long before he had it taken away from him by Llywelyn ab Iorwerth. In the year 1240 the English won the castle from the Welsh, who took it back, so it is not very clear to which century the supernatural happenings described by local people belong. The Prince Dafydd might be the one whose skull stands in Ffangallt Farm, near Holywell, where he was murdered.

About fifteen years ago two ladies were visiting Ewloe Castle and had climbed up to the upper ward over the ruins of the curtain wall, when all at once they saw a bright dancing light making its way across the curtain wall and into the main tower, known as the Welsh Tower. It wound itself around this Tower in a snake-like way and then seemed to enter one of the only two window slits remaining in the south wall.

They left at once, frightened by this strange light. Both were certain it was not a reflection. It seemed to have a will of its own. It certainly was not someone directing a torch. There was no sun shining at the time, and later they thought that a U.F.O. might have passed through the Castle.

There have been reported sightings of U.F.O.'s in Wepre Park within the last few years. Some of the sightings were not really of a U.F.O., but the object clearly visible was a man-made American Satellite which used to pass over Wepre Park for some years, its visibility becoming fifteen minutes later each night. The appearance of this satellite used to be mentioned every evening in the Liverpool Echo.

The next reported strange occurrence around Ewloe Castle took place some nine years ago.

Two young men one summer evening went for a walk up to the Castle just as it was getting dusk. At that time there was no constructed path as there is now from Wepre Woods to Ewloe Castle, only a rough woodland path with a climb up the red rock to reach the Castle. Just as they reached the precincts of the Castle they heard the sound of marching feet which were not quite in step. Immediately the Alsatian dog with them started to whine and shiver. The sound of the marching became louder and louder and was accompanied by the sound of music. It could have been harp music but the tune was not a known ancient Welsh air and they were unable to recognise it. They were not at all frightened, they said, only filled with curiosity. They said that they had heard that the Celtic armies of centuries ago marched with Bards who sang warlike songs to the harp accompaniment to encourage the marchers and inspire them to victory.

The late Mr William Brown of Chester Road, Shotton, to whom they told the tale of the marching feet and music, was very interested. He said that a friend of his, shortly after the First World War, had climbed up to Ewloe Castle and on his way he heard the sounds described by the young man, but also failed to see anyone.

The two young men have often since walked up through Wepre Park to the Castle in the evening, but have never again heard the marching feet and music.

WAS IT THE MIST?

Through the years many people have told tales of sightings of the White Nun of Wepre Park, Connah's Quay.

This park was once the grounds of a Welsh Mansion, but never had anything to do with nearby Ewloe Castle, and was called Wepre Hall. Eventually, about forty years ago the local council purchased the old Hall and there was a sale there of all the beautiful panelling, etc. Much of this has found its way to several private houses in the area. Until a few years ago there was a massive Council tip behind the ruin of the old Hall, and there is now a Council Depot where part of the old Hall stood, but it is fortunately screened by trees. The remains of the old pond in the grounds were dredged and stocked with coarse fish by a local Angling Society, and this is very popular and well maintained. This year a Visitors' Centre has been constructed on the old site of the hall.

There have been at least two suicides in the pond. The head of a murdered woman was found by the pond a few years ago.

Two or three years ago, about seven o'clock on a June morning, a young boy was fishing in this pond; there was no-one else around but this did not worry him.

The boy had just caught a fine big roach and was bending down to put it into a keep net when he sensed someone near him, although he could not see any shadow. On looking up he saw on a strip of ground in the centre of the pond, the figure of a lady dressed in white who stared at the boy. The air had all at once become deadly cold like the worst day in winter. She rose in the air and floated across the water towards the bank he was fishing from. For a few seconds he was rooted to the spot from sheer terror. When he was able to move he ran towards the main park, forgetting all about his new fishing gear left on the bank. To his relief he saw two men coming towards him near the park gates. He stopped the men, who were surprised at the state he was in. The boy told them what he had seen and asked them to go back with him to the pond to collect his fishing gear, as he was too terrified to go back by himself.

Laughingly, they agreed to go with him, saying he had been imagining things and that the figure of the white lady was probably a trick of the mist as it moved across the surface of the pond.

This did not convince the boy, who was sure he had seen a ghost, but he did not argue with them, being much too shaken. When they reached the side of the pond he quickly picked up his property. He and the two men turned around to go back when in front of them stood the ghostly figure which stayed in sight for about three minutes then vanished. The men no longer laughed and now they really thought they did see, "The White Lady of Wepre Park".

There are no records of a Priory or Convent having been sited in this particular area of Wepre.

The apparition might have been that of the daughter of a Welsh Chieftain, one of the Felyn family, who lived during the 12th century in Northop, some two miles from Wepre. Her body was interred in Northop churchyard, and her tombstone still stands.

AN ANCESTOR PAYS A VISIT

This tale will surely make the reader think.

My stay in the hospital bed seemed very long. It was a wonderful hospital, Barrowmore, Cheshire, closed about three years ago. I was under very specialised nursing care.

I was seriously ill and getting worse and overhead the Registrar discussing amputation of my left arm and part of the breast. One of the wonderful Sisters said, "Not if Sister X and I know it! We do not like pieces cut off our patients."

There I was, floating in and out of consciousness day and night — for me time had ceased. There seemed to be strings of burnt ragged streamers below the ceiling of the ward. It was Christmas but I did not know.

I must have been in hospital for three months when something unforgettable happened. One particular night the moonlight streamed through the long ward when something caught my eye. Underneath a window opposite me there appeared to be a crouching figure. I was not afraid. I called a nurse. "There's an old man huddling over there. Can you see him? He is almost like a tramp but he is harmless, I know. Do you think he is hungry?"

"No, you're dreaming. Hush dear, you will scare the others. Try to sleep again."

She walked away and I looked again. He was still there. Now I saw his face clearly; it was kind and he was smiling so sweetly. He appeared familiar and seemed to be trying to tell me something. He wore a countryman's smock in the fashion of about two hundred years ago. On his head was what looked like a hat made of straw, fairly high crowned. He had a book tucked under his arm. It looked like a Bible. Oh, where had I seen him before? He had a look something like my late father, with penetrating light blue eyes. He gave another smile and vanished. In that instant I knew I was going to live. I fell into a natural sleep.

It took another four months of staying in hospital, then a few more confined to bed at home.

A year later an acquaintance of mine, writer Marjorie Howe, sent me a copy of her book "A Georgian Drop out". It was the biography of Richard Robert Jones — Dic Aberdaron, near Pwllheli, North Wales. Dic was a man reputed to have taught himself fourteen languages. He received only three years normal schooling. Born in 1790, he died in 1843. He was an eccentric who travelled between Aberdaron, Lleyn, and Liverpool. Sometimes he was accompanied by a tabby cat. Great scholars were proud to call him friend. At times he was entertained lavishly by them. He was obviously exploited by clergymen and professors plagiarising his work. His main admirer and kind patron was statesman and Liverpool scholar William Roscoe.

Many of Dic's translations from Greek, Hebrew and Latin are lost, and most of his dictionaries. His Welsh, Greek and Hebrew dictionary is his only preserved work. It was never published, and the manuscript is in St Asaph Cathedral Library. He is buried in St Asaph Cathedral cemetery. Eminent scholars from all over the world have during the long years visited the Cathedral to see his grave and look at his manuscript.

It has been said he was a magician and a story is told that he reaped a field at Caer Eos, his first home in Aberdaron, in about an hour.

When he uttered impreciations in various foreign languages upon those who had offended him, he scared the superstitious. He did read magic books, but only for academic knowledge. To keep himself fed he very occasionally foretold the future, but hated having to do that.

Shortly after I returned from hospital I received Mrs Howe's copy of her book. On the cover was an illustration of the little man I had seen that night in hospital.

Here is a secret now disclosed. I am on both sides of my father's family a direct descendant of Dic Aberdaron. The family, like most Victorian Methodists, did not want to know about Dic. I am proud to know he was one of my ancestors. I had no idea what he had looked like. When I told Mrs Howe of the ghost I had seen and described it, her book was still at that time at the printers until its publication in 1978. I had, on oath, never seen the portrait owned by William Ross of Dic Aberdaron, or any other of him. She was as surprised as I was, but had to believe I had either seen his ghost or a vision.

Why did he appear to me? I started to recover from that moment, so was it E.S.P. on my part, because I certainly possess it at times?

My father, either because he did not want to (or did not know) never told me anything of interest about Dic. "We thought he was a sort of tramp," he said. "He died long before I was born. I had heard he was a scholar," he went on.

Shortly after he died my father's own spirit appeared to enable me to obtain help to save my baby's life. She was taken seriously ill in the night, and I got her to hospital just in time. That account appears in the Author's *Welsh Ghosts, Poltergeists and Demons*.

THE DOGS OF WEPRE PARK

During the late nineteenth century and this century right up to about two years ago, a group of dogs were said to haunt the grounds of Wepre Park, Connah's Quay, fairly frequently at twilight and during the nights. The number in the pack increased and decreased through the years.

In Welsh folklore there are many tales of the Dogs of Darkness, in Welsh *Cŵn Annwn*. They were said to hunt souls for their Master Satan as well as being omens of disaster.

The hounds differed in colour: one pack would be black, with red glaring eyes; another pack was white in colour with red ears and eyes; a third pack consisted of part-coloured hounds. The height of every dog was four feet tall and their baying was dreadful to hear.

The dogs of Wepre are all shapes, sizes and colours and resemble from tiny King Charles' Spaniels to Deerhounds. The people who claim to have seen them state every dog was grey coloured in the moonlight. It is like the French stating, "All cats are grey at night." The dogs of Wepre bark, yap and yelp. None have ever been heard to howl or bay, like the *Cŵn Annwn* are supposed to do.

Owners of the Mansion of Wepre who lived there during Victorian and Edwardian times were great animal lovers and used to bury their dead pets in separate graves with headstones bearing the pets' name. For years in the summer local residents were allowed on Sundays to take a walk around the "Dog's Graves" as they were known locally.

Sadly, about twenty years ago the graves began to be vandalised, until now not a stone remains. Vandalism has been the fate of the children's swings, seesaws and the pensioners' seats from time to time. Enough to make any ghost haunt the Park, and they have — according to the old folks' tales about the Park.

The late Mister William Brown, a local historian, told me that about fifteen years ago he was taking his dog for an evening stroll across the Park when it started to whine and cringe. It would not move from his side and suddenly the sound of barking filled the air, and in the bright moonlight Mr Brown saw a crowd of dogs rushing towards him. This was too much for his dog who whined loudly and nestled close to him. The dogs ignored him and hurried off towards the ornamental pond in the Park. They wheeled round and made towards the Dogs' Graves, where they disappeared from sight. Up to the present there is only one wide vehicular exit from the Park and the dogs (said Mr Brown) certainly, did not leave through it.

After the dogs had vanished there came the sound of wailing from the direction of the Dogs' Graves. After that first occasion Mr Brown said he saw the phantom dogs running around the parkland in the moonlight a few times.

Nearly four years ago, a young couple were excercising their two dogs on a light night in June. They were walking along a pretty woodland path which ran parallel to what was once the walls of the Dogs' Graves, when the two dogs, normally aggressive to challenging male dogs, began to shiver and shake and, like Mr Brown's dog, cowered to the ground.

Out of where the gravestones used to stand a pack of large and small dogs jumped out, howling madly. They raced past the terrified couple and made for a pond named the Rosy, where they vanished but no splashing sound was heard.

The couple left hurriedly, pulled along by their two dogs who were still shaking, and left by a small gate near the pond.

They kept the phenomenon to themselves for a few weeks in case anybody laughed at them and said they had imagined the sighting of the spectral dogs.

BIBLIOGRAPHY

Aubrey John, *Miscellanies*, London, 1696.
Archaeologia Cambrensis, Journal of the Cambrian Archaeological Society, Various Editions from 1846.
Black Book of Carmarthen, J.G. Evans, 1906.
Barddoniaeth Dafydd ap Gwilym, 1789.
Baxter, *Certainty of the World of Spirits*, London 1691.
Bingley's Tours of North Wales, Volumes One and Two.
Borrow George, *Wild Wales*, London, 1901.
Bygones, *Wales and the Border Counties*, Oswestry, 1871.
Celtic Folk Lore Welsh and Manx, Prof. Sir John Rhys, Oxford, 1901, Two Volumes.
Cambrian Popular Antiquities, Peter Roberts, 1815.
Cambrian Superstitions, William Howells Tipton 1831.
Complete Collection of Cymru Coch Magazine, Ed. O.M. Edwards 1891-1927.
Cymru Fu, Ed. Isaac Foulkes, Liverpool 1862-1864.
Edmund Jones, *Apparition of Spirits in Wales 1780*, Trefeca.
Y Genhinen Quarterly Magazine 1883 to 1928, Caernarfon.
Giraldus Cambrensis Itnerarium Kambriae et Descripto.
J.F. Dimock, *Kambriae*, Rolls Service, 1868.
Iolo MSS Various, from Iolo Morgannwg's Collection.
Mostyn Manuscripts, National Library of Wales.
Pennant's Tours of Wales, Three Volumes 1883.
Parry The Vitae Merlini, Latin Text with Translation, University of Illinois Press 1925.
Drych yr Amseroedd, The Work of Robert Jones Rhoslan (Dic Aberdaron) published as part of *Y Llenor*, Wrexham 1898.
Marie Trevelyan, *Glimpses of Welsh Life*, London 1904.
Marie Trevelyan, *Snowdon to the Sea*, London 1905.

ACKNOWLEDGEMENTS

The author gratefully acknowledges the assistance given her by the undermentioned:-
Clwyd County Librarian, Mr Gwyn Williams.
Assistant Clwyd County Librarian, Mr A. Watkin.
Deputy Librarian and Museums Librarian, Miss Dwynwen Roberts.
Mrs Cynthia Ankers, County Librarian's personal secretary.
Mr D.R. Hughes, Local History Librarian Clwyd.
Mr Hedd ap Emlyn, Welsh Book Librarian, Clwyd.
Mr T. Spence, Senior Librarian Clwyd.
Mr Dennis Roberts, Mr Mike Hill and Mr J. Thomas, Librarians Clwyd.
Miss Carol Moseley, Librarian, Clwyd.
All members of H.Q. Library staff for their infinite patience and to the telephone staff.
Clwyd County Archivist, Mr Geoffrey Vesey.
Clwyd County Assistant Archivist, Mr C.J. Williams.
Mr T. Mathias, Ruthin Senior Records Officer.
Mr Bryn Parry, Gwynedd County Archivist.
Gwynedd County Assistant Archivist, Mrs Ann Lovell.
Mr G. Mc Cormick, Sen. Master, St. Richard Gwyn High School, Flint.
Mrs J. January, Treuddyn.
Mr D. Philphot, Headmaster, St. Richard Gwyn High School, Flint.